A HISTORY OF
AMERICAN
HIGHER EDUCATION

A HISTORY OF
AMERICAN
HIGHER EDUCATION

By

PAUL WESTMEYER, Ed.D.

Professor of Higher Education
The University of Texas at San Antonio
San Antonio, Texas

CHARLES C THOMAS • PUBLISHER
Springfield • Illinois • U.S.A.

Published and Distributed Throughout the World by

CHARLES C THOMAS • PUBLISHER

2600 South First Street

Springfield, Illinois 62717

© *1985 by* CHARLES C THOMAS • PUBLISHER

ISBN 0-398-05083-X

Library of Congress Catalog Card Number: 84-16315

Printed in the United States of America
Q-R-3

Library of Congress Cataloging in Publication Data

Westmeyer, Paul.
    A history of American higher education.

    Bibliography: p.
    Includes index.
      1. Education, Higher—United States—History.
I. Title.
LA226.W45 1985   378.73   84-16315
ISBN 0-398-05083-X

PREFACE

HIGHER education in the United States can probably be described as vocationally oriented. Certainly not all institutions have as their major purpose the preparation of graduates to assume specific (or generic) jobs; there are liberal arts institutions and also liberal arts degrees in more general institutions and these, traditionally, do not include job preparation as a major goal. Nevertheless, research studies have found that by far the major purpose of the students in colleges and universities is to end up with better jobs than they would be able to obtain if they did not have college degrees. A report in the *Chronicle of Higher Education* in early 1982 quoted Alexander Astin as having found in a major survey of freshmen at 368 colleges that 65% of students surveyed set "being very well off financially" as a very important goal of their college education (compared with 49% who expressed this goal in the 1969 survey).*

The first colleges in this country were actually vocationally oriented, too, since their major purpose was to prepare ministers for the associated churches (or perhaps it would be more correct to say that the purpose was to prepare an "educated clergy"). However, the psychology of the times was such that training of the mind became a more general, more important, and more pervasive purpose of the colonial colleges before very long in their history. As a matter of fact, it became very difficult for leaders to install vocational programs in colleges very early in our development, as we shall see. Benjamin Franklin, practical person that he apparently was and strongly favoring the education of the people in practical matters (witness his

---

*"This Year's Freshmen Found Oriented toward Financial Success," (*The Chronicle of Higher Education*, Feb. 17, 1982).

"Juntos," a very early form of continuing education for adult citizens, with their emphasis on discussions to improve citizenship), was nevertheless in favor of the classical curriculum in colleges. Thomas Jefferson wanted to incorporate into the University of Virginia a vocational possibility, in that students could elect the courses they would take. However, this election was (a) only between schools, that is, the student was free to choose which of the available schools he would attend (there were eight — ancient languages, modern languages, mathematics, natural philosophy, natural history, anatomy and medicine, moral philosophy, and law), for degree-seeking students or (b) truly free, that is, a student could take any course he chose if the goal was not to obtain a degree. Within the schools the degree programs were fixed and they were also highly classical.

The young United States (even before it was the United States and was referred to as "the American Colonies," or more simply as "America") was a very practical country. There was little time for the "foolishness" that German universities were engaging in — research — and so it was a long time before the university came into being here. Strangely, though, the real practical area that one would assume our forebears would have been concerned with — agriculture (and a bit later industry) — was not a part of the early institutions of higher education in this country. As a matter of fact, the two areas mentioned came into prominence only after the Civil War in universities that grew out of the Morrill Acts.

So, higher education in young America (the title of this book uses "America" rather than "United States," not because the book is intended to encompass higher education in all of North, Central, and South America of today, but rather because "America" of our early history really meant the colonies that gave rise to the United States) was, perhaps, somewhat unusual. It was vocational because of the practicality of the population, but it was not related to the basic activity of most of that population. It was, or became, liberal (in the sense of mind training) in what was really a very non-liberal setting. As we shall see, it was narrowly religious in a country that began because of religious oppression. Although in many ways it was patterned after institutions in the "mother countries" of those who began higher education in America, it remained unlike the major institutions, the universities, for some long time. What were the causes of these and many other uniquenesses in our history?

While the major purpose of this book is to provide an account of our higher education history, the highlights, the milestones, the major developments, the great changes both within higher education and outside but related to higher education, and to describe in some detail the nature of selected institutions, their operating arrangements, and their influences, there will also be some attempts to relate the developments in institutions to those in the country at large. The "frontier colleges" provide one natural example of this; since the country was really moving at the frontier in a geographical sense it had to happen that special colleges were developed at appropriate geographical locations and with appropriate purposes to match this movement. Of course, there is also the fact that evolution in one existing college almost inevitably influenced changes in other colleges. To what extent did the great plans and arrangements that developed at Wisconsin influence the structure and functioning of Illinois, or Purdue, or Iowa? Did the state universities have any major influence on the private universities or was Chicago actually the model for all of them? Some of these questions will be examined and answers may or may not be forthcoming.

This book is not the result of an historical research study. Of course, a lot of reading of historical accounts has preceded its writing, but the data from this reading has not been assembled and analyzed as it would have been in a research project. Also, unlike the procedures that I would have followed in a research project, I have not gone back to original documents but have relied upon secondary information (and have trusted those secondary sources). Consequently, this book is not intended for the research scholar but rather for the general student of history, the student of higher education, the professor of either of these, and anyone who is interested in learning more about our antecedents in this country.

I write as I talk (or is that *like* I talk?) and this is sort of informal. I never mean to be flippant and I certainly revere the individuals who contributed to our history in higher education; however, some of their actions, viewed in today's light, do appear strange, and I may say so at times. Try to ignore such comments, if they disagree with your own views, and read the book for its intended purpose, as an historical account that attempts to put together the events that seem important into a chronological description of higher education in America.

Although I have avowed that this is not the result of a research study, I have given credit to those references from which I took information in a specific way. The only way in which I can give credit to all the other sources that I read is to acknowledge here that there was a large number of them and to thank their authors collectively. I must also give credit to my students in higher education classes; surely the greatest motivator, as well as the most powerful process, for learning is to attempt to teach others.

P.W.

INTRODUCTION

EDUCATION is timeless. Higher education, as a separate institutional arrangement, can be dated in some ways. Socrates was
a higher educator, if you will, and the so-called Socratic method remains not only a viable but also a desirable procedure for the instruction of adult learners — especially if the instruction is in thinking areas rather than in skill areas. Plato and Aristotle can also be
pointed to as prominent teachers as well as outstanding scholars and
it might be interesting to notice throughout the account here presented how much, or even whether, scholarship and teaching are
tied together. From these Greek scholars there did develop certain
traditions that are still entrenched in higher education. From the
Greeks in general we inherited the categorization of disciplines, the
trivium (grammar, rhetoric, and logic — and aren't these still the
fundamentals in our college general studies curricula?), the quadrivium (arithmetic, geometry, astronomy, and music), and the professions (law and medicine). The quadrivium was the course of study
between the equivalent of a bachelor's degree and a master's degree
in the medieval universities, and we shall see how it entered into the
American colleges, as well. And, of course, most modern universities (or at least university systems) have associated with them a
school of law and a school of medicine, as well as other professional
schools more recently developed. So one could date some aspects of
higher education to somewhere around 300-400 B.C.

In the Catholic church the monasteries certainly have had a lot to
do with higher education, as centers for learning, as locations for
book copying before the invention of the printing press, and as
sources of thought stimulation (remember, Martin Luther was a
monk). The earliest record of a monastery is around A.D. 330 and the

location was on the Nile River. We have no specific effects of this monastery on higher education, but in A.D. 528 St. Benedict did codify schooling under the 73 article Rule of Benedict; the codification included specific reading requirements following the trivium and the quadrivium and also included church history and canonical law. Some two centuries later Charlemagne (A.D. 742-814), while encouraging the continued development of monastic schools, established what might have been the first private school, a palace school for the education of the sons of noblemen; was this an early separation of church and state education?

From the ninth until the seventeenth centuries A.D. scholasticism was the dominant philosophical movement and, within this movement, there had developed by the twelfth century A.D. major monastic schools. In these schools the basic teaching procedure was that the teacher read material and the learners copied it down (shades of lectures and notetaking in today's universities). However, there had also developed by this time the procedure known as disputation, which was primarily a debate using logic more prominently than factual information. Disputation found its way into the early American colleges. Following the Crusades, Aristotelian science was introduced into the teachings of scholasticism through the efforts of returning crusaders who had learned it from the Saracens (who controlled Spain at that time). Logical science played an important role in colonial curricula; experimental science entered the curricula only with great difficulty much later.

During this period of gradual evolution schools came to be centered at cathedrals (the natural locations for basically religious training) and they became more and more organized. Eventually, in the same way that unions developed in America, guilds were formed within the schools for protection against those who might seek to regulate them — kings, bishops, etc. Before long the basic guild separated into student guilds and teacher guilds. (Guilds were *universitas*; teacher guilds were *facultas*.) As organization continued the facultas elected *deans* as their heads and the student guilds elected *councilors*. What would be more natural than that the deans and councilors, the guild leaders, should form a *council* and elect a sort of supreme head, a *chancellor*? So, there was in the cathedral schools of Europe an organization not totally unlike that which exists in American universities today.

Remember, these were church schools and, despite the guilds, they were still controlled by the church and by the individual who was head of the particular church. The schools were allowed to operate (*chartered*) by that church head — a king, an emperor, the pope — depending upon the location of the particular school. And the chancellor was given the authority to issue *licentia docendi* ("teaching licenses") to qualified students. You see, the basic reason for becoming educated in a cathedral school was to become able to educate others, so the "degree" was certification that you had acquired the information and skills necessary to instruct others. A few of the largest and most prominent schools were given authority to issue *licentia docendi ubique*. Note the forerunners of bachelor's degrees in the basic license and of master's or even doctoral degrees in the "ubique" license. Note also the terminology we have adopted from the cathedral schools — university, faculty, dean, council, chancellor; in one school, Bologna, the student guilds actually controlled the operation and the guild *rector* headed the school; hence, we sometimes call our university head a rector today.

From the cathedral schools it was as simple as making a name change to have a city school. Of course, once the change was made the character of the school began to change also. The University of Salerno (ninth century A.D.) was among the earliest of the city universities; the University of Paris (ca. A.D. 1160) became the greatest of them, encompassing some 40 colleges in its organization. Oxford was modeled after the University of Paris (A.D. 1167) and, as hinted above, succeeded in having looser papal supervision than prior schools had. (In A.D. 1209 a group of Oxford scholars became dissatisfied with the operation of that school and founded Cambridge University. We shall see this very thing happen also in the colonial colleges of America.)

Earlier I pointed out the antecedents of our present-day basic degrees; actually there was in Europe an even closer set of forerunners. In the twelfth century A.D. students studied until they could demonstrate proficiency in Latin in the areas of study; at that point they were termed *bachelors*. After 4-7 more years of study, when they had learned to dispute effectively and had developed and defended a "masterpiece," they became known as *masters* (meaning teachers). The whole practice developed from the need for a clergyman to: (1)

be able to thoroughly understand Latin writings and (2) be able to defend religious doctrine against anyone who might disagree with it. We, of course, still carry on the tradition of requiring a defense of the doctoral dissertation (the "masterpiece") if not of the master's thesis in modern universities.

The Renaissance (fourteenth through seventeenth centuries A.D.) in Europe was a period of speeded up changes in politics, religions, economics, and in education. Also, the arts grew tremendously and the humanistic influence of the arts affected this evolution. During this period secularism continued to grow in education and the Catholic church was effectively "unseated" as the manager of higher education. (Martin Luther lived A.D. 1483-1546 and John Calvin A.D. 1509-1564; of course, there were many others who contributed to the changes — Gutenburg invented the printing press in A.D. 1450.) After Luther's death, Protestantism became splintered and grew even faster and larger than before and this growth had a profound influence on higher education. This influence was centered in Germany. In Luther's day the German universities were subject to protectors (usually dukes) who ruled the area in which they were located. In the states of Saxony, Bavaria, Thuringia, Brandenburg, etc., there were the universities of Leipzig, Munich, Erfurt, etc. Luther had been a professor at Erfurt and at Wittenberg. As the beliefs of protectors varied and as the political unrest in Germany grew from the religious unrest (started through the normal practice of debate, by the way), the universities came to be the stable institutions. After all, a protector could proclaim certain beliefs, but information remained the same, or essentially the same, despite beliefs. The German universities had by this time become respected seats of learning and this respect only grew through the unrest.

The German universities had a great influence upon American institutions. The essential freedom to discover new information, to do research, known as *lehrfreiheit*, is one of these influences that is still profoundly visible here. The whole movement toward academic freedom carried by the AAUP (which we will learn about much later) was based on this idea. And the *wissenschaft*, investigation and, more importantly, writing (publishing) is also prominent in today's higher education systems in this country. Actually, the *lehrfreiheit* was the idea that new knowledge was valuable whether or not it made a contribution to everyday life; the counterpart for students was *lernfreiheit*, the freedom to learn what one desired and, at least in part, this idea had an influence upon our elective systems. Interestingly, Laurence Vesey* suggests that the German universities were not really as America saw them. The research, while it may have been scientific at times, was more likely to consist of philosophical examination of ideas or of rather loose collection of data. (There did develop in the German universities, however, a tradition of painstaking attention to details in a study and, of course, this has become a part of formal research procedures universally utilized.)

Finally, I would be remiss in not mentioning in this introduction that there were no less than ten universities in Central and South America prior to the opening of Harvard. The two oldest of these were the Royal and Pontifical University of Mexico and the University of San Marcos in Peru.[†] Both were established in A.D. 1551.

So, with this background we now turn to American higher education and begin the accounting of its history.

P.W.

---

*Vesey, Laurence R., *The Emergence of the American University*, (Chicago: University of Chicago Press, 1965), pp. 125 ff.

[†]Brubacher, John S. and Willis Rudy, *Higher Education in Transition*, (New York: Harper and Row, Publishers, 1976).

CONTENTS

A HISTORY OF
AMERICAN
HIGHER EDUCATION

CHAPTER 1

THE FIRST COLONIAL COLLEGES

IN December of 1606 Captain John Smith (26 years old at the time, short, bearded, and hot-tempered) set out with a group of potential colonists for America. They came in three ships: the *Susan Constant* (largest at 100 tons displacement), the *Godspeed* (40 tons), and the *Discovery* (20 tons). They landed at Jamestown in May 1607 with the goal of "conquering Virginia." By 1622 some 6,000 colonists had arrived, but only about 2,000 of them had survived. These were not the Puritans (they came just a bit later and it was that group of dissatisfied emigrants from England who, perhaps partly due to their dissatisfaction, saw the need for an institution of higher education in the new world). The Jamestown colonists had come for different, more economically based reasons, and perhaps this differing background did not require continuing higher education.

The colony to which the Jamestown settlers came (Virginia) had been chartered by the English Royal Crown to the London Company and so was a private venture. However, in 1624 King James I revoked the charter and the settlement became a royal colony. Under private management the colony had not done well, but as a royal colony it prospered and, as we shall see, opened the second of the colonial colleges in America.

The group of religious dissenters (and they were truly dissenters, as part of the body were known as "Separatists") who came to be called Puritans left England in 1608 to settle temporarily in Holland. How this came about and how some of the group ended up in America is an interesting story.*

---

*Information taken from Feenie Ziner. *The Pilgrims and Plymouth Colony*. (American Heritage. the Magazine of History. Harper and Row distributors. 1961).

3

Following the Reformation in Germany, there were wars and shifts of allegiances in European countries. Holland ended up as a completely Protestant nation by 1648. France remained embattled, although the Huguenots were granted partial freedom for a time. England vacillated. King Henry VIII separated the country from Catholicism and proclaimed himself the head of the Protestant Church in England (eventually to be known as the Anglican Church) and his son, Edward VI, enhanced this stand. However, the next ruler (Edward's half sister, Mary) proclaimed a return to Catholicism and the following queen (Mary's half sister, Elizabeth) returned to Protestantism once more. The church retained many of the Catholic rituals (and added some of its own) and those who read the Bible carefully were unable to find a basis for many of these practices. When they protested that the church should simplify its operations, they were sneered at, and when they insisted that the church must return to its former *purity*, they came to be called Puritans, derisively.

During this period of stormy arguments, Cambridge was a stronghold of Puritanism. Four of the Puritan leaders studied there: William Brewster, Robert Browne (so violent in his opposition to the Anglican Church practices that he urged separation of his followers from the mother church and his followers thus became known as Separatists), John Penry, and John Greenwood. It was Browne who led a group of Puritans to Holland. In 1593 both Greenwood and Penry were hanged for their heresies. Brewster met a young man named William Bradford who was part of the Puritan movement in a sort of quiet way at the time and took him into his home; both hoped that the Puritan cause in England would be helped by the new ruler, James I (who had been James VI of Scotland and who was the son of Mary, Queen of Scots). However, James believed in the divine right of kings and resisted any moves that might diminish his own power. (He also had a fiery temper and reacted harshly when the Puritans proposed that one of their rights was to choose their own ministers rather than have them appointed.)

Among the good results of the Puritan "rebellions" in England was the translation of the Bible into the beloved King James Version. The Puritans had suggested that a new translation was desirable (in 1604) and James took up this suggestion and assigned some

50 scholars to the work. The new translation was published in 1611 but was never accepted by the Puritans who continued to use the Geneva Bible, a Calvinist translation.

Brewster, Bradford, and their fellow Puritans bravely separated themselves from the mother church in defiance of King James and they determined to flee to Holland. Anticipating that they could not receive permission from the king to emigrate, the Puritans attempted to leave England stealthily. They failed in 1607 but, after many harrowing adventures, managed to reach Amsterdam in 1608. There not all was as peaceful as expected. The new arrivals were stricter in their interpretations of the Scriptures than the earlier arrivals and quarrels broke out between the groups. Brewster, Bradford, and the bulk of the Separatists moved to Leyden in 1609. Holland turned out also not to be as safe as the Puritans had hoped. There were rumors of impending conflict with Spain (and return of the inquisition). There were temptations in Leyden for the youth of the Separatists who saw the Hollanders enjoying the sabbath in ways that were forbidden them. The Puritans found it difficult to make a living in their new homeland. Brewster himself ran a printing press and some of his publications resulted in condemnation by King James, who demanded his return to England (Brewster hid out). All of this led to discussions about another move — to the New World.

Meanwhile, the English colony at Jamestown, Virginia had essentially failed. Many of the colonists had died and new settlers were wary of going there; James I had even offered pardons to condemned men if they would go to Virginia. Under these circumstances the Puritans decided that it would be very likely that they could obtain permission to emigrate to America and to settle in the Jamestown area. However, James I was willing only to say that he would not molest them if they sailed, not to grant them royal permission. In the midst of the bargaining some of the Amsterdam Separatists did set sail for America, but the voyage was ill fated and only 50 of the original 200 Pilgrims arrived alive. Negotiations continued, with the Puritans remaining interested in a location that would get them out from under the English crown; New Netherland was considered. Eventually, however, it was an English company (the Merchant Adventurers) that provided the way for the trip to the New World. It was this company that proposed to finance the trip and to settle the group in Northern Virginia where they could take up the fishing trade.

On July 22, 1620, sixteen men, eleven women, and nineteen children left Leyden aboard the *Speedwell* for Southamptom, where they were to join the *Mayflower* for the voyage to America. The Mayflower passengers, however, were Anglicans (not called by that name yet), not Puritans (or Separatists); the group, incidentally, included John Alden, Priscilla Mullins, and Captain Miles Standish. It also included a small child, Mary Allerton, who eventually was to be the last of the Mayflower survivors. The *Speedwell* turned out to be unseaworthy and so all the passengers crowded aboard the *Mayflower*, which finally left England on September 6, 1620.

Land was sighted on November 10, 1620, but it was Cape Cod and the pilgrims did not have "patents" to land there. The ship's crew wanted to return to England as quickly as possible, so they urged the passengers to go ashore. Amidst the general unrest the Mayflower Compact was drawn up and signed by those men of the company who were eligible; this compact represented an agreement of self-government and John Carver was elected as the first governor of the colony. After several exploratory trips, it was decided to settle at Plymouth (the famed landing on Plymouth Rock on December 21, 1620, was the third of the exploratory trips). The *Mayflower* left for England; Governor Carver died, and William Bradford was elected governor in his place. Following a severe winter, the Pilgrims prospered in the new year, and during the summer they sent their ship (the "longboat" from the *Mayflower* which the Pilgrims had retained for their use) on a trading expedition to the Massachusetts Indian country near what would become Boston. It was in this year that the celebration that is now known as Thanksgiving Day was held, with a group of Indians invited to join the settlers in a feast.

In the years following, the settlers of Plymouth spread out and founded several additional towns. New shiploads of Pilgrims arrived and these new arrivals tended to settle in new locations, also. Meanwhile, civil war in England had resulted in the emigration of new groups of Puritans which included such shrewd businessmen as John Endecott and John Winthrop. Endecott obtained a royal charter for settlement of territory between the Charles and the Merrimack Rivers (his group arrived at Naumkeag, founded earlier by the expanding Pilgrims, took it by force, and renamed it Salem). Winthrop became governor in the Massachusetts Bay Company under which some 1,000 settlers came to America in 1630. Boston, Dorchester, Medford, Watertown, Roxbury, and Lynn were quickly established and the new settlers, by force of numbers, basically absorbed the earlier ones. The new settlers were convinced, however, that the ways of the Pilgrims were right in the election of officials and in the practice of religion following the Separatist insistence upon breaking with the Church of England. The Massachusetts Bay settlers were both Puritan and democratic.

In 1624 the Pilgrims had planned to open a school because they believed strongly that it was the duty of every man to learn to read the Scriptures for the glory of God. Numbers (small) and lack of financial stability prevented them from actually beginning the school. However, by 1636 there were enough settlers in the Boston area and the finances of the region were stable enough that Harvard College could be opened.

As I said earlier, Boston was founded in 1630. The Puritan religion, which was essentially anti-Anglican in its beliefs, served as the guide for all activities in the settlement. Governance of the colony was by "freemen," members of the Puritan Church, who elected a governor and representatives to the General Court. Ministers, of course, were prestigious but, nevertheless, were under the control of the freemen, their parishoners. It was in this atmosphere of intolerance, with respect to religious beliefs and of influential clergymen who were still slightly under suspicion by the freemen, that Harvard was founded. But we will come back to that in a short while.

Due largely to Puritan intolerance, settlement of Massachusetts spread outward from Boston, although the bulk of the new settlers was still Puritan. In 1635, Thomas Hooker, one of the Puritan ministers, left Boston to found a new town, New Haven, and in 1662 he obtained a royal charter for the new colony, called Connecticut. Connecticut was basically Puritan, although it was somewhat more liberal than Massachusetts. It was in this more liberal atmosphere that Yale was founded, the third of the colonial colleges.

The colony of Connecticut had been peaceably settled as the result of disagreements over religious principles; Rhode Island, however, came into being because of a more serious rebellion. Roger

This is misleading; too simplistic ←

Williams believed so strongly in individual rights that he insisted upon two major changes in the operation of Massachusetts: (1) church and civil affairs must be separated, and (2) land taken for use by white settlers must be purchased from the Indians. The basic Puritans could not tolerate these demands and so Williams was banished from the colony. With his followers he moved to an area that eventually was chartered as a separate colony in 1644, called Rhode Island and Providence Plantations. It was in this still more liberal atmosphere that the school that was to become Brown University was founded.

Meanwhile, the French had settled Quebec (1608) and the Dutch, New Netherland (1609). Killiaen Von Rensselaer, a Dutch merchant, had brought 50 settlers, which was the requirement for obtaining a land grant, and had established a colony in what is now New York. Quakers had settled in Pennsylvania (1681). In 1732 Georgia was chartered by England. In 1752 the trustees abandoned the charter and Georgia became a royal colony, also.

The Puritans, although bigoted and intolerant of other religions, were committed to careful examination of their own beliefs. They detested "ignorant sinners" for both reasons — ignorance and sin. They insisted upon educating their children and they considered a learned ministry vital to the community. In 1633 John Eliot proposed, in a letter to the General Court, a college for Massachusetts Bay. Harvard Colledge (its first name was so spelled) was established by the General Court in 1636, instruction began in 1638, and the college charter was set by the General Court in 1650. The school was named after John Harvard, who contributed the land upon which the buildings were placed and donated his own library to get the college library started. Physically, there was a college hall, a library, offices, and a grammar school. Organizationally, the college was patterned after Emmanuel College of Cambridge University. There were four classes: freshman, sophomore, junior sophister, and senior sophister and the bachelor's degree thus required four years of study. In addition, there were plans for an advanced degree (a master's degree), but these will be discussed later.

Any person who aspired to be admitted as a student at Harvard had to be able to: translate any of the classics into English, read and write Latin in both prose and poetry, and perfectly decline the paradigms of nouns and verbs in Greek. However, residents who desired to live and eat with the fellows of the college, but who either did not want to be scholars (regular students) or were ineligible for admission, could obtain this privilege by paying double tuition. Such special persons were called fellow-commoners.

The program of study included: reading the Old Testament from Hebrew into Greek, being instructed in Hebrew, being "led through" all the liberal arts, and participating in weekly declamations and public disputations. When the four years of study had elapsed and the scholars had been examined in the "languages and sciences" that they had studied, they were awarded the degree of bachelor. After an additional three years of study, composing "synopses" of the liberal arts and participating in public disputations on questions of a higher level than those at the bachelor's level, a scholar could receive the degree, master of arts.

The Harvard Charter of 1650 spelled out the organization of the college as consisting of a corporation including the president, five fellows, and a treasurer or bursar. This corporation was to be called "The President and Fellows of Harvard College" and was to be self-perpetuating. It carried all the authority needed for the college to operate, fixing a seal, appointing officers (instructors, etc.), purchasing property, receiving gifts, suing and being sued, and investing monies. However, in language which is not totally clear to today's reader, the charter also provided for overseers, who were to "allow" decisions made by the corporation, "consent" to actions taken by it, and make decisions in cases of nonagreement among the corporation members. The overseers consisted of six magistrates and six ministers. Henry Dunster was the first president, and the initial corporation had only two fellows and a treasurer.

Dunster remained president until October 1654, when he resigned and was replaced by Charles Chauncey. (The overseers had tried to get Johannes Commenius as president, but he declined.) The occasion of Dunster's resignation involved the rather fierce religious philosophy of the school. Dunster had come to believe some of the teachings of the Anabaptists, particularly those having to do with

adult baptism and baptism by immersion. It was said that he had become engulfed in an "unhappy entanglement in the snares of Ana-
baptism."* This Puritan school could not endure such heresy, fearing
that the students might also become ensnared in it, and so the overseers asked Dunster to resign.

Another early problem involved the balance between the corporation and the overseers. Apparently, the fellows of the corporation were initially teachers (tutors) in the college, but this practice
was deviated from in that several fellows were elected who were also
on the board of overseers. This gave the overseers a stronger influence on the actual management of the college than some of its
constituents considered appropriate. In 1727 the General Court
tried to reduce the power of liberals who controlled the corporation
by replacing three liberal ministers with three tutors. Nicholas
Sever, a tutor who wanted to become a member of the corporation
and who had a reputation as a troublemaker at the college, proposed
that it had been the original intent of the charter that fellows should
be tutors anyway. Sever's argument did not carry the day and it became more clear that fellows could, indeed, be nontutors, and if
there was overlap with the overseers this was not prohibited.

Later on, a new charter for Harvard College was proposed but
was disallowed by the English king; thus, Harvard did not receive a
royal charter but remained under its original charter. Under that
charter a leader of the overseers, John Lowell, was instrumental in
delineating the internal and external management functions, and so
the overseers moved toward a lay governing board and the corporation toward the faculty governance body that Tutor Sever had
wanted.

Shortly after the initial settling of Virginia, the new farmers discovered tobacco. It grew readily in Virginia and could be sold profit-
ably in England. The colony quickly freed itself from dependence
upon subsidies, the Land Company outgrew its usefulness, and its

---

*Quoted from Cotton Mather's History of Harvard, 1702, Item 5. In Richard Hofstadter
and Wilson Smith (Eds.): *American Higher Education: A Documentary History*, (Chicago: University of Chicago Press, 1961, vol. I).

charter was revoked in 1624 by James I. Then came the English Civil War and, under Cromwell, little change occurred in the new world. In 1660, with the restoration of Charles II to the throne, however, England again began to expand colonization (into Carolina). Meanwhile, the Puritan religion had suffered ups and downs, with a general decline that perhaps culminated in the counterreformation that led to the Salem witch-hunts of 1692. Thereafter, Anglicanism and other religions became much more widespread in America. The era was also one of mercantilism. The Dutch had come to monopolize sea trade with America until, in 1650, the English Parliament barred non-English shipping. (The Navigation Act of 1660 even restricted the goods that could be shipped outside the empire.) By 1691 England had new leadership, the cousins William and Mary.

The new rulers granted a royal charter to the second colonial college, William and Mary College, in 1693. The college was proposed by James Blair, Anglican Church head in Virginia. In structure it was modeled after Queen's College of Oxford University. It had a board of trustees (at first) and a faculty with separate powers, but the charter directed dissolution of the trustees over a period of time. The actual statement was that the trustees, as soon as the college had become established, were to assign all the property rights to the "President and Masters" of the college. In 1729 the directed move was carried out and the trustees became a board of visitors, while the faculty became essentially the governing body of the school. Following the Revolution, however, Virginia courts denied faculty autonomy (the royal charter being no longer in effect) and the visitors regained more authority. Thomas Jefferson proposed even more state control for the institution but was thwarted; he then moved to found the University of Virginia in competition with the older school, his alma mater.

The College of William and Mary, in Virginia (its full name in the charter), had schools of philosophy and divinity and an Indian School. (Due to the evangelistic nature of the early colonial religions most of the colleges of the day had as one of their major purposes the conversion of American Indians to Christianity.) It also had a grammar school to prepare applicants. There were two types of scholars, self-paying and those supported by the college. The financial support came mostly from a tobacco tax authorized to the college in the charter; later there was also an export duty on skins and furs and a tax on peddlers (1759). Despite being "state" supported, the college was strongly religious. The president (James Blair had been appointed its first president — for life) was required to be Anglican as were all of the masters. Furthermore, the president was also to be head of the Anglican Church in Virginia.

The "Collegiate School in Connecticut," which became Yale College, had a rocky beginning. Chartered by the colony in 1701, it had no permanent location; it operated in at least five different towns (at one time in three of them simultaneously). Increase Mather had been president of Harvard and his son Cotton aspired to succeed him. This did not happen, however, and in 1716 Cotton Mather wrote to Elihu Yale, a Boston-born member of the East India Company (and rich), suggesting that he consider supporting the college that had been chartered 15 years earlier and hinting that if he did so the college might name itself after him. Yale did donate approximately 550 pounds; the college was then built at New Haven and took the name of its benefactor. Cotton Mather was appointed president.

Yale was a reformed Puritan college. Its purpose was to "protect the faith of the fathers," but the era and the location both allowed much greater theological diversity and philosophical deviation from previously accepted truths than was true at Harvard. The new school had 36 students in 1710 and had grown to 338 by 1770 (in the same years Harvard had 123 and 413 students). The school had been founded without a royal charter and the congregational (i.e., Puritan) clergymen who had sponsored it were leery of the struggles between Harvard's overseers and the corporation, so in the charter for Yale (actually just the legislation that established the school) they set up a single board, the unicameral Yale Corporation. In 1748, Thomas Clap, who was then rector of Yale, persuaded the Connecticut General Court to issue a formal charter for the college. In this charter, which still governs the school, the primary operating body was the president and fellows of Yale College in New Haven. The college president (name changed from rector) was thus on the governing board. The board was self-perpetuating; fellows could be removed or added by vote of the board itself. In practice the board was a *lay* board and not the internal management board that the Harvard Corporation became.

Harvard and Yale were Puritan colleges; William and Mary was Anglican. There were other faiths also growing in America, although Anglicanism tended to be the official religion. The farther on the frontier people were located, generally the more distant from the approved faith were their beliefs. Thus, New Jersey became heavily Presbyterian, except for the southern region which was Dutch Reformed. (Rhode Island had become largely Baptist by the mid 1700s.) The College of New Jersey at Princeton was chartered by King George II of England in 1746 to serve primarily as a Presbyterian seminary. (The 1746 charter is known only from a newspaper advertisement; there is a confirmatory charter dated 1748.)* Despite its obvious religious orientation, Princeton (later name) was not to exclude "any Person of any religious Denomination whatsoever from free and Equal Liberty and Advantage of Education, or from any of the Liberties, Privileges, or immunities of the Said College on account of his or their speculative Sentiments in Religion and of his, or their being of a Religious profession Different from the said Trustees of the College."†

Harvard, William and Mary, and Yale were avowedly religious. Remember that President Dunster had to leave Harvard for his Baptist beliefs. In 1745 John and Ebenezer Cleveland were expelled from Yale for having abandoned their assigned chuch meetings to attend those conducted by an unorthodox minister. Professors at William and Mary had to subscribe to the thirty-nine articles of the Church of England until the American Revolution. Princeton broke the mold by allowing persons of any religious faith to enter as students, and the remaining colonial colleges were even more liberal; Brown even refused to exclude sectarian differences from the course of instruction. The country was not yet ready for academic freedom (it wasn't even a free country yet) but the movement was in that direction.

---

*Tewksbury, Donald G., *The Founding of American Colleges and Universities Before the Civil War*, (New York: Archon Books, Teachers College, Columbia University, 1932).

†Quoted from Charters of the College of New Jersey (Princeton), 1746, 1748, Item 17. In Richard Hofstadter and Wilson Smith (Eds.): *American Higher Education: A Documentary History*, (Chicago: University of Chicago Press, 1961, vol. I).

It is significant that William Livingston opposed the founding of sectarian (Anglican) Kings College in New York. He was a Whig leader in the Revolution later on, but what he wanted at the time was a religiously free college set up by the civil authorities and under civil supervision rather than church supervision. Nevertheless, Kings College, which became the University of the State of New York, then Columbia College, and finally Columbia University, was founded as a sectarian school in 1754. Its curriculum, however, included surveying, navigation, husbandry, mineralogy, geography, commerce, and government (hardly sectarian subjects, although these broad listings apparently bore little fruit in the form of actual courses).

This survey is scant at best; inaccurate at worst!

By 1752 the French and English in America were at war. In 1756 the conflict spread to Europe and later became known as the Seven Years' War. During and after the war, England tightened controls on its colonies. A whole series of taxes were imposed without colonial representation in Parliament. In 1765 nine colonies met together in the Stamp Act Congress. By 1768 Samuel Adams was proclaiming that England had no legislating rights over the colonies. England dissolved the Massachusetts legislature and sent troops to Boston; in 1770 the Boston Massacre occurred; in 1773 the Boston Tea Party precipitated even more severe restrictions imposed by England upon its colonies. In 1774 Massachusetts called for a meeting of delegates from all the colonies; this meeting became known as the First Continental Congress, and Georgia alone was not represented. King George III declared the New England governments in a state of rebellion and sent troops, again, to Boston. War between England and Massachusetts began before the Second Continental Congress met in May, 1775.

It was during this immediate pre-Revolutionary War period that the remaining colonial colleges were founded in America. The first actual non-church college was the College of Philadelphia which became the University of Pennsylvania. Benjamin Franklin had proposed plans for a broad practical kind of education in a 1749 pamphlet. Four years later a Scotsman, William Smith, migrated to America and published his ideas on education, which included:

without colonial representation!

- two "courses" — the traditional classical one and a second course for the mechanics profession,
- all instruction to be given in English,
- the inclusion in both courses of science, surveying, history, agriculture, English, writing, speech, and contemporary politics.

Franklin read the publication, liked what it said, and invited Smith to preside over the new college in Philadelphia which opened in 1755. American colleges were beginning to respond to American needs, not to English requirements, and to frontier thinking rather than to traditional thinking.

Rhode Island College was founded as a Baptist institution in 1764 at Providence. In 1795 its president and corporation resolved that for a donation of $6,000 anyone could name the college. Nicholas Brown donated $5,000 and was allowed to give his name to the school, which eventually got $160,000 of his fortune. (Many of the American colleges that bear now-familiar names were given those names in honor of donors in the same manner: James Bowdoin — Bowdoin College, William Denison — Denison College, Henry Rutgers — Rutgers University, William Carleton — Carleton College, Washington Duke — Duke University.) As had been the case with preceding colleges, the charter of Brown exempted faculty members from paying taxes. This was a sore point with the populace and attempts were made to change it. In 1863 the college and the state agreed to exempt a maximum of $10,000 of real estate from taxes for each faculty member, and following World War II the Brown faculty voluntarily gave up this exemption, also. The college was open to students of all religions, but it was managed by a very precisely stipulated board of trustees. In perpetuity there were to be 22 Baptists on the board, 5 Friends or Quakers, 4 Congregationalists, and 5 Episcopalians. The fellows also must include 8 Baptists, with the remaining 12 being from any denomination. The president was to be a Baptist.

Queens College was opened in Brunswick, New Jersey in 1766 by the Dutch Reformed Church (a Presbyterian body). It was, however, nondenominational in its admission policies. Queens College became Rutgers College and later Rutgers University. Following passage of the Morrill acts (see later section) it became the "A & M" college for New Jersey, as did Brown for Rhode Island, Dartmouth for New Hampshire, part of Cornell for New York, and part of Yale for Connecticut.

The last of the colonial colleges, Dartmouth, was founded in 1769. The founder was Eleazar Wheelock, who was supported by the Congregationalist Church which had been unable to make any inroads at Puritan Harvard and Yale. ("Congregationalist" was the name for the newer or reformed Puritan Church.) Wheelock obtained a royal charter from England in spite of the very near break between America and the mother country. The charter provided for a self-perpetuating board of trustees and for a president who was to appoint his own successor. This circumstance eventually gave rise to the landmark *Dartmouth College* case (1819).

As provided in the charter, Eleazar Wheelock appointed his son John as his successor. However, John was a military man, not a cleric, and he came to dispute some of the teachings of the Congregationalists; later, in the same dispute, he also lost control of his faculty. The college trustees removed him from the presidency and from the board of trustees and dismissed him as a professor as well. In public appeals, Wheelock enlisted the aid of the "less privileged" Republican Party, and in the 1816 election a Republican governor was elected in New Hampshire. Under the new governor the legislature passed a law changing Dartmouth College to Dartmouth University and bringing it under state control. The trustees brought the case to court; meanwhile, both the trustees' Dartmouth College and John Wheelock's Dartmouth University (he had been reinstated in the same legislation) operated at Hanover, New Hampshire, for about a two-year period.

The basic question in the case was whether the school was a public or a private corporation. The Supreme Court of New Hampshire ruled that it was public, that the trustees were responsible to the people, and that the whole matter was therefore under legislative control. The case was appealed to the United States Supreme Court. Daniel Webster argued the case before the court presided over by Chief Justice John Marshall. Webster made the case one of contractual soundness and private rights.

> This, Sir, is my case. It is the case not merely of that humble institution, it is the case of every college in the land. It is more. It is

the case of every eleemosynary institution throughout our country...the case of every man who has property of which he may be
stripped — for the question is simply this: shall our state legislature be allowed to take that which is not their own, to turn it from
its original use, and apply it to such ends or purposes as they, in
their discretion, shall see fit? Sir, you may destroy this little institution...but if you do...you must extinguish, one after another,
all those great lights of science, which, for more than a century,
have thrown their radiance over the land.*

The Supreme Court in a 5-1-1 decision decreed that Dartmouth
College was not a public institution, that it was not under public
control, and that its charter was a contract which could not be
changed without the agreement of the corporation that the charter
established.

In his opinion in the Dartmouth College case, Chief Justice John
Marshall said that there was little doubt that the charter that created
a college was a contract and also no doubt that if the institution were
a "civil" one or if the funds with which it operated were public funds,
then the state of New Hampshire would have rights of regulation
over the college. However, he said that if the institution were an
eleemosynary one and held privately donated funds for its use, then
those who gave the funds had a right (even though they may be no
longer living) to expect the institution to operate exactly as it was
outlined in its charter. (After all, donors gave money on the basis of
the charter description in the first place.) The question, he said, was
not whether or not there could be an institution of higher education
founded by a government and under control of that government,
but rather whether or not Dartmouth College was such an institution.

He went on to say that the charter set up a corporation with "im-
mortality," that is to say that it was perpetuated by the succession of
individuals who administered its provisions. The trustees were not
public officers but private ones and the institution then was not a
public one but private. In his view, had the charter been recalled the
day after it was granted, there would have been an outcry that a sacred contract had been violated. And, he said, nothing had hap-

---

*Quoted from Daniel Webster Argues the Dartmouth College Case, 1819, Item 14, Part
III. In Richard Hofstadter and Wilson Smith (Eds.): *American Higher Education: A Documentary History*, (Chicago: University of Chicago Press, 1961, vol. I).

pened to change that; altering the charter at this later time would have the same effect.

Making a second point, Chief Justice Marshall said that another question was whether the acts of the New Hampshire legislature, which changed the nature of Dartmouth College in effect, had impaired the original contract (charter). He said that such actions prior to the adoption of the United States Constitution would have been suspect, but after that adoption they were clearly inappropriate. The Constitution provided that a state legislature may not pass acts that impair the obligation of contracts. Under the New Hampshire legislation, Dartmouth College would have been made subject to the civil authorities of the state; in Marshall's words, "the will of the state (would be) substituted for the will of the donors, in every essential operation of the college."

The court's judgment, then, was that the New Hampshire acts were unconstitutional, that judgment should have been in favor of the plaintiffs (Dartmouth College trustees), and that the judgment of the state court was to be reversed. Dartmouth College remained as it had been and was not transferred to state control. Wheelock's Dartmouth University ceased to exist.

The court decision in this case apparently delayed the founding of state universities some 50 years, although it did not say that state control of educational institutions was improper. What did result immediately from the decision was a spurt in the founding of small colleges (the era between about 1820 and 1870). What also resulted from the decision, in a more long-term fashion, was the confidence of boards of regents in their right to manage colleges without interference from civil authorities.

These then were the colonial colleges: Harvard (1636), William and Mary (1693), Yale (1701), Princeton (1746), Columbia (1754), University of Pennsylvania (1755), Brown (1764), Rutgers (1766), and Dartmouth (1769). Among the thirteen colonies, New Jersey had two colleges and Delaware, Maryland, North Carolina, South Carolina, and Georgia had none. Except for Delaware, each of these colonies did establish one or more colleges soon after the Revolutionary War; the following list completes this picture:

Washington College, Chestertown, Maryland (1782)
University of Georgia, Athens, Georgia (1785)
College of Charleston, Charleston, South Carolina (1785)
University of North Carolina, Chapel Hill, N.C. (1789)
Newark College, Newark, Delaware (1833)

And finally in other New England states there were:

University of Vermont, Burlington, Vermont (1791)
Bowdoin College, Brunswick, Maine (1794)

Reviewing the management and organization of these colonial institutions, the early European schools were essentially managed by guilds of masters (teachers) and of scholars (students) that eventually united to form a sort of corporation (a universitas). The pope, emperor, king, or elector protected, and thus to an extent could prescribe for, the school but he did not manage it. With the Reformation, however, lay control of the church developed and this rather naturally led to lay control of colleges.

The models for American colleges were Dutch and English. The University of Leyden (Holland) had a board of curators appointed by the estates general, the civil authorities, and an academic senate composed of the resident professors who were appointed by the curators. English universities had chancellors who actually had little authority, but English colleges had heads, usually called headmasters, who actually governed the colleges.

In colonial America, Harvard had a board of overseers, with the president of the college on the board and a corporation consisting of the president and fellows. President Dunster apparently wanted the corporation to hold the most power, but the charter actually gave it to the overseers. As mentioned earlier, William and Mary also had a board-faculty arrangement, but the board was intended to decline in authority. Yale was more Dutch in its organization. At first the Yale Corporation, a lay organization, did not even include the college president, although it did include him after 1745. The University of Pennsylvania followed the Yale pattern as did most of the other colonial colleges — strong board and no or little faculty authority. (In planning the University of Virginia Thomas Jefferson did not even include a president, having a rotating faculty chairman instead.)

The college president taught (as colleges grew he taught only the senior class), administered discipline, preached at chapel and also preached on Sunday, kept student records, kept the library, raised funds, and handled the day-to-day business of the school. His titles were master (early Harvard), president (later Harvard), rector (early Yale), provost (University of Pennsylvania), or principal (Dickinson). All presidents in colonial colleges were clergymen.

The Harvard Corporation was composed of the president, five fellows, and a treasurer. In practice, after the very beginning, vacancies on the corporation were filled by tutors until 1723 when eligible tutors were passed over and local clergymen were elected instead (see earlier comments on the *Sever* case). This nonprofessional, lay membership idea grew with increasing lay control of all college operations. Around 1826 there finally developed the idea of lay control through a board of trustees, which managed external and financial matters, and faculty control through faculty senates or similar organizations that managed internal matters.

Following the Revolutionary War the financial situation of colonial colleges became difficult and many appealed to the states for assistance. The basis for private support of the colonial colleges was pledges of subsistence — mostly pledges of produce rather than of money — and actual money was scarce. (Kenyon College was supported for a time by "Kenyon Circles of Industry," which were sewing circles, and this support was, fortunately, in the form of cash, but not all colleges were as fortunate, especially the colonial colleges.) In 1789 the General Court of Massachusetts appropriated funds to help support Harvard and these continued until 1823. In order to obtain similar support, Yale had to undergo some drastic governmental changes.

Ezra Stiles was president of Yale from 1778 until 1795; he had been a tutor there and before that a student. (As a graduate of Yale during this period, of course, he was a Congregational minister.) He did much to move Yale toward scientific research in an era prior to Darwin; the research at the time was more logical and searching than it was speculative and experimental — as a matter of fact there was probably none of the latter — but it was, nonetheless, scholarly.

Stiles was a scholar. During his presidency there was a need for additional funds and the question arose of adding laymen to the corporation to facilitate the acquisition of state assistance. Stiles reported on this in 1792.*

At first the suggestion was made only that a couple of persons be added to the corporation, but Stiles reported that by 1777 he had become convinced that nothing short of a majority of members on the corporation would satisfy the state and result in financial help from that source. Stiles himself felt adamantly that the majority of the corporation must remain clergymen. It was suggested that the governor, lieutenant governor, chief justice of the superior court, and speaker of the house be added and Stiles objected to the chief justice on the grounds that there could be court cases involving the college and there would be a conflict of interest. He also asked if an equal number of clergymen and laymen would satisfy the state and was told that it would. Stiles at that time remained adamant that the corporation must continue to have at least two-thirds "ecclesiastics" (as he called them). The faculty, too, feared a "takeover" by "civilians" and stood behind Stiles.

Finally, the legislature passed a resolution to add funds to the college ($30,000) if there were added to the corporation the governor, the deputy governor, and six more "civilians." And the corporation voted to accept this offer with a quorum to consist of four civilians and six ecclesiastics, and with the corporation to perpetuate itself except for the civilian members. (There were eleven members of the corporation in the original charter.)

Harvard and Yale had both avoided royal charters (although Harvard did try to obtain one later) in order to keep their management private. William and Mary welcomed a royal charter, since it included a provision for the college to name two members to the House of Burgesses and thus gave the college some say in public affairs in exchange for having a measure of public control on its own

---

*The following information was taken from Ezra Stiles on Changes in the Yale Corporation. In Richard Hofstadter and Wilson Smith (Eds.): *American Higher Education: A Documentary History*, (Chicago: University of Chicago Press, 1961, vol. I).

activities. The board of regents (using today's terminology) of Yale was originally self-perpetuating, but in 1763 certain enemies of president Clap pressured the legislature to appoint visitors "more responsive to the colony's interests." President Clap argued that the colony had no such rights, since the school existed before the "state" chartered it. He won, but as we have seen it was a temporary victory, since the need for state support caused Yale to accept public figures on its governing board. We have come through more evolutionary stages to today's boards of regents, which are primarily political in makeup.

CHAPTER 2

COLLEGES IN YOUNG AMERICA

THE Constitution of the United States of America was drafted in 1787; ratification proceeded as follows:

Delaware (1787)	South Carolina (1788)
Pennsylvania (1787)	New Hampshire (1788)
New Jersey (1787)	Virginia (1788)
Georgia (1788)	New York (1788)
Connecticut (1788)	North Carolina (1789)
Massachusetts (1788)	Rhode Island (1790)
Maryland (1788)	

The United States was now a free country, but it was far from free of abuse by European powers. Between 1793 and 1794 about 600 U.S. ships were seized by France and England. John Jay's Treaty of 1794 (with England) obtained some compensation for the seized ships but, more importantly, England agreed to evacuate her outposts in North America west of the United States. The Spanish, afraid of a possible English alliance with the United States, then conceded navigation rights on the Mississippi River and settled the Florida boundary dispute. American settlers poured westward. Kentucky became a state in 1792, Tennessee in 1796, and the Mississippi Territory was acquired in 1798 and the Indiana Territory in 1799.

Politically, this was the era of the great debate between Hamiltonian aristocratic government ideas and Jeffersonian democratic republican ideas. Hamilton, of course, died in a duel with Aaron Burr in 1804. Jefferson had become president in 1801, having been chosen over Burr by Hamilton's vote. By 1812 we were again at war with England. Major universities founded during this period were:

Washington and Lee (originally Liberty Hill Academy),
Lexington, Virginia (1782)

University of Tennessee (originally Blount College),
Knoxville, Tennessee (1794)

Ohio University (originally American Western University),
Athens, Ohio (1802)

Miami University, Oxford, Ohio (1809)

University of Maryland, Baltimore, Maryland (1812)

Georgetown College, Washington, D.C. (1815)

By 1819, when the University of Virginia was founded (it was Central College 1816-1819), the United States included, in addition to the original thirteen states, Ohio, Indiana, Illinois, Kentucky, Tennessee, Alabama, Mississippi, Florida, Louisiana and the territories of Arkansas, Missouri, and Michigan, plus the Oregon Country occupied jointly with England. Maine was still a part of Massachusetts. One-fourth of the U.S. population was beyond the mountains from the original East Coast settlements.

The Declaration of Independence, in a statement based on the ideas of John Locke, insisted that all men are created equal. (Locke: [1] There are no innate ideas, the mind is blank; knowledge comes from experience. [2] Knowledge is tentative and partial; thus tentative judgments, tolerance of the opinions of others, and freedom of inquiry are essential to learning. [3] A man should be judged by what he does, not by what he is.) The American ideal included the belief that progress is possible rather than just maintenance of the status quo, that the general good is best served by allowing each man to work first for his own good, that all men are capable of reason and that environment (especially education) influences the use of reason, and it insisted in the Constitution that church and state must be separate. All of these principles, plus those that grew out of the Dartmouth College case, greatly influenced college development in the period between the wars, 1776-1861.

During this time over 800 colleges were established in this country, but only 180 survived to 1900. Most were pillars of some establishment — church, political order, or social convention — but most also included a rather heavy introduction of secular studies. The United States Military Academy opened in 1802 (more details, along with information on other military schools, will be given later), Rensselaer Polytechnic Institute in 1824, Massachusetts Institute of Technology was chartered in 1861 and opened in 1865; Harvard, Yale, Dartmouth, and Brown all added technical schools to their programs, as did the University of Pennsylvania.

Shortly after 1800 American private colleges again began to find themselves more and more in financial difficulty. In particular, their growth was impeded by a lack of growth funds, although their day-to-day operations might have been able to continue. In 1848 President Edward Everett of Harvard appealed to the Massachusetts legislature for funds to buy scientific apparatus. He said that the growth of the sciences necessitated maintaining a constantly updated set of materials and apparatus for student use; the Lawrence Scientific School had just been opened and was in sore need of assistance. At the same time, however, Everett pled for funds to build the library collection, also. The library had over 53,000 volumes at the time, but Everett said that many of them were practically useless, having been donated without regard to how they would fit into the collection. What Harvard needed was a working library, but it did not have sufficient funds to build one. The plea did not result in state funding.

In the following year, Everett again asked the legislature for money (one-half million dollars) to support the college. His argument was based on the fact that the state did support public schools (one million dollars worth), but persons who wanted a college education had to pay for it totally themselves. He suggested that a college education for more citizens would be advantageous to the state and that if the state provided funds more students could be induced to take their work at home rather than going abroad for it. Thus, the rich who were already in college (but often in Europe) would tend to go to Harvard, while many others who were less affluent but able could also obtain local degrees.

The University of Georgia was chartered by the state in 1785 with a self-perpetuating board of trustees and a board of visitors that consisted of the governor, the speaker of the house, the chief justice, and the "state councillors." It also was supported through a land grant of 40,000 acres. However, sectarian influences on the board of trustees managed to counteract any real state surveillance until 1881 when the school actually came under state management.

Similar events occurred in South Carolina and North Carolina. In Delaware, a state-controlled board of trustees (to be elected by the legislature) was set up for Delaware College in the charter of 1821. However, the opening was postponed indefinitely when religious groups objected. The Presbyterians obtained a charter for Newark College in 1833, with a self-perpetuating board, repealing the 1821 charter. In 1843 this school became Delaware College and attempted to serve the secular needs of the state, but it did not really become a state school until 1913 — and the University of Delaware in 1941.

It was first in Virginia, then, that state control of the university was actually achieved. There was no less religious opposition to a state school in Virginia than there was in other states, but Thomas Jefferson was so powerful that his ideas succeeded where others had failed. The opening of the University of Virginia is generally ascribed to 1825, but its first charter (as Central College) was established in 1816, and this was a revision of an even earlier charter that had not actually given rise to the "academy" it authorized. Central College became the University of Virginia in 1819, with a board of visitors appointed by the governor. The school was to "in all things and at all times be subject to the control of the legislature." It was supported with state funds. The curriculum was to include English, mathematics, government, agriculture and commerce, science, and "reasoning and reflection." To be admitted students should first have graduated from a "college"; this did not mean the same thing that it does today, however, since the University of Virginia was not a graduate school but only a broadly comprehensive practical and philosophical institution. It needs to be made clear, further, that the several institutions that had been founded to this date that were called universities were not universities in either the graduate school sense or the research sense. Of course, the programs in American colleges were broadening, becoming more practical, and at the same time becoming more liberal, but the development of true universities remained for a later time.

Thomas Jefferson's University of Virginia might well have been the first true university in America had its programs operated as intended and had it actually borne the fruit that its potential provided for in the planning. Under Jefferson's ideal the institution would have both diffused knowledge and advanced knowledge.* The university was divided into eight schools — ancient languages, modern languages, mathematics, natural philosophy, natural history, anatomy and medicine, moral philosophy, and law — and each school had a professor at its head (at the beginning this professor was the *only* one). Students were free to choose which schools they would attend (in effect an elective system) and the university itself offered no degree; each school awarded its own diplomas. (The latter circumstance was a rather effective deterrent to the elective system nominally in place, since a student who desired to obtain a diploma was bound to attend a particular school and not jump around among them. The result was that the system was elective for "degree students" only insofar as that they could choose among the schools; for non-degree students the system was truly elective.) Thus, the foundation was laid for a university in fact, multiple "colleges," research as an expectation of professors, "*lernfreiheit*" for students, and, at least nominally, graduate study possibilities. With regard to the last of these, the University of Virginia began awarding the M.A. in 1831, having abandoned the no-degree plan; there is some doubt (according to Rudolph) that the level of study was truly beyond the usual B.A. level, but the degree was, nevertheless, an M.A. In actual practice it is doubtful that Virginia was truly a university until after the Civil War.

VIGNETTE

THOMAS JEFFERSON (1743-1826)

> Thomas Jefferson was a member of the aristocracy of Virginia, a planter and a surveyor. Having been privately tutored, he studied mathematics at William and Mary (with science as a second field) and he then became a lawyer through an apprenticeship program. At the age of

---

*Frederick Rudolph, *The American College and University, A History,* (New York: Vintage Books [Random House], 1962).

34 he was the primary writer of the Declaration of Independence (Benjamin Franklin, John Adams, Roger Sherman, and Robert Livingston were also on the drafting committee, but Jefferson, at the urging of John Adams, wrote the actual draft). In 1779 he was elected governor of Virginia. He was the Republican candidate for the United States presidency in 1796 but lost to John Adams and became vice-president. The election of 1800 was the famous one that gave rise to the Twelfth Amendment to the United States Constitution. It was in this election that Jefferson became president but only after 35 deadlocked votes in the House of Representatives. During his presidency, the northwest expansion was begun and the funding of education through devoting to school support one section of land of every 36 sections surveyed was initiated.

Religiously, Jefferson was a Unitarian (a tolerant body); he believed in the separation of church and state. Politically, he was an aristocrat, although he believed in democracy. He was against higher education for women, although he did believe that women should be educated "appropriately." Jefferson was against the practice of sending American youth to Europe for their education. He felt that it was more appropriate for them to be locally educated. Thus, he wanted a public university when he proposed the University of Virginia. (His actual idea of an educational system for Virginia had William and Mary at the top as a university to cater to the best of the bright students. At the bottom there was three years of general education for everybody (at public expense). Next was the grammar school for the "bright poor" (the bright rich could attend academies), then six years of study for the best of the bright students, and finally the university for the very best students only. When he failed in his efforts to make William and Mary into a university as he envisioned it, he proposed the University of Virginia.)

The University of Iowa claims to have been founded on Jefferson's ideas, also.

Meanwhile, public schooling in America was also developing. Webster's "spellers" and "readers" were produced beginning in 1783. Elementary schools were established by federal land ordinance in 1785. In 1821 the Boston High School for Boys opened, and it is very likely that the *colleges* referred to in the records of the University of Virginia were similar to this school — preparatory schools that were intended to get boys ready for entrance into a college (or a "university"). Massachusetts, ever the leader in things educational it seems, passed a law requiring the maintenance of public high schools in 1827. The funding of public schools in the country was sort of "in the air" for several years — until the Kalamazoo decision in 1872 established the legal right of school systems to tax the public for the support of high schools.

The Horace Mann School, a "normal" school (meaning a teacher preparatory school), was opened in 1837 in Lexington, Massachusetts. However, this was not a college-level institution; normal schools later became colleges, of course, but initially they were at the high school level. In 1841 the first of the "model schools" (later called laboratory schools) was established as part of a normal school. Federally, the U.S. Bureau of Education was established in 1867. One of its first duties became that of deciding which of the many institutions of education in the country were properly to be called colleges. (The Association of American Universities also became involved in this matter, as did the accrediting agencies, but we will come back to this later.) The first list of "colleges" for the country included all 369 institutions that granted degrees.

Frederick Jackson Turner, a professor at the University of Wisconsin (ca. 1900), proposed an idea which he called the "Frontier Thesis." The idea was that American social development had experienced and was continuing to experience a continual "beginning over" on the frontier. Whatever institutions and practices had developed in older communities were not simply adopted by frontier communities; rather, frontier practices and institutions tended to emulate older ones and simpler ones and so the evolutionary process repeated itself in each frontier location. Thus, the New England colonial colleges were much simpler and "older" in form than their European models. So, too, the 800 colleges of the 1776-1861 era were simpler and older in form than their own East Coast models. They were small, mostly denominational, narrow in curriculum, and they had low standards. Given the head mastership of an elementary or high school, many teachers aspired to making that school into a college — and they often succeeded. Little wonder that so many of the colleges of this era failed in the competitive evolution of higher education.

However, there were two classes of frontier colleges that tended to belie the frontier thesis. The "Yankee colleges" were deliberately patterned after specific Eastern institutions, with Yale, Princeton, and Harvard being the primary models. There were at least sixteen "Yales of the West," including Western Reserve (Cleveland, Ohio, 1826) and Beloit College (Beloit, Wisconsin, 1846). Emory College (Atlanta, Georgia, 1836) was a frontier "Harvard." Some 25 colleges, including a few state universities, patterned themselves after Princeton.

The second different group of frontier institutions was comprised of those few forward-looking state universities that really strove to meet local needs and also to look to the future at the same time. Among these one can point to Indiana University (Bloomington, Indiana, 1828), the University of Michigan (Ann Arbor, Michigan, 1837), the University of Wisconsin (Madison, Wisconsin, 1848), the University of Minnesota (Minneapolis, Minnesota, 1851), and the University of California at Berkeley (founded as the College of California in Oakland, California, 1855). The University of Michigan had a unique beginning and we will return to this shortly.

Amherst College was founded in 1825, Kenyon (Ohio) in 1826, Wesleyan in Connecticut in 1831, Denison (Ohio) in 1832, Hanover (Indiana) in 1833, DePauw (Indiana) in 1837 as Indiana Asbury University, the University of Kentucky as Bacon College in 1837, the University of the State of Missouri in 1839, Notre Dame in 1844, the University of Mississippi in 1844, Bucknell, Colgate, and Fordham all in 1846, Tulane in 1847 as the University of Louisiana, the State University of Iowa in 1847, Earlham and Butler (both in Indiana) in 1850, Tufts in 1852, Duke (as Normal College) in 1852. Vassar Female College opened in 1861 in Poughkeepsie, New York. Texas founded 40 pre-Civil War colleges, but only two of them survived — Baylor (at Waco, 1845) and Austin College (at Sherman, 1849).

VIGNETTE

FRANCIS WAYLAND (1796-1865)

> Wayland's B.A. and M.A. in medicine and theology were from Union College (Schenectady, N.Y.), and he became a tutor at that institution as well as a Baptist minister (First Baptist Church of Boston) in later years. He returned to academia (Union College) in 1826 and a year later was selected to be president of Brown University. He immediately dismissed all non-resident faculty and replaced them with residents. His views were quite conservative and he believed in the use of public libraries as the primary mode of public education.

The *University of Michigania* was established according to a plan conceived by Augustus Woodward, who was a judge in the Michigan Territory. The founding legislation also refers to the university alternately as the *Catholepistemiad*.* The institution was to have 13 professorships (called *didaxiim*), the first a professorship of catholepistemia or universal science and this professor was to be president of the university. Then there were professorships (didaxiim) of anthropoglossica or literature, of mathematica, of physiognostica or natural history, of physiosophica or natural philosophy, etc. The organization was set up to include on the one hand the president and didactors as the legal entity to run the institution and a board of trustees and visitors to "watch over the interests" of the institution. The Catholepistemiad had rough sledding at first, perhaps because the state maintained too heavy a hand in its operation. However, in 1850 the board of trustees and visitors was reconstituted as a board of regents that were to be elected as an additional branch of the state government rather than being under the legislature. This independence, along with the leadership of Henry Philip Tappan as president of the university, eventually led to Michigan's assuming an outstanding position in higher education. Tappan viewed higher

---

*Establishment of the Catholepistemiad, 1817, Item III, Part II. In Richard Hofstadter and Wilson Smith (Eds.): *American Higher Education: A Documentary History*, (Chicago: University of Chicago Press, 1961, vol. I).

education in the German style: a university at which knowledge was not only dispensed but also determined, lesser branches under this university to serve as feeders of students to the head institution, and at the bottom of the pyramid the system of public high schools and elementary schools.

Tappan had a profound influence on the University of Michigan, although much of this influence did not show up until after his dismissal from the presidency of that institution. The Catholopistemiad had opened in Ann Arbor in 1841 and Tappan became its president in 1852. He had a vision of a graduate institution, saying that there should be two levels of activity at the school, a lower level for those still learning how to learn and an upper level for those who knew how to learn (and, presumably, how to create new knowledge). His vision followed the pattern of the great German universities which were in favor with the "intellectual elite" in America (they sent their sons there for graduate study) but not with the "rank and file" (they felt that America did not need such presumed high-level institutions, it needed more practical ones).

Tappan was successful in convincing his board of regents that his ideas were correct and appropriate for Michigan. Indeed, the board decided officially that when there was a demand, courses would be offered in the new areas being taught in Europe and at the higher levels. However, the legislature which had to supply funds for whatever the University of Michigan did was not convinced of the worth of Tappan's ideas, nor was the press. Tappan was not a tactful man and he did use wine, although commonly not to excess, and this later turned out to be his formal undoing. Initially, it was these along with his outspokenness and his political views, that led to his unpopularity among the public. Internally, Tappan was also able to convince a sufficient number of his faculty that the university idea was correct for Michigan that his plan was voted into effect; this was in 1855. In 1857 the regents formally approved a plan for advanced study that would culminate in an *earned* M.A. or M.S. degree, but only small numbers of students took advantage of the new offerings.

Since the Catholepistemiad was totally state supported, its offerings were subject to the whims of politicians and the public and, of course, to the management of its board of regents. In 1858 the board of regents that had been friendly to Tappan retired and was replaced with a new board that quickly became antagonistic to the new ideas. Thus, the university was unable to develop along the lines that Tappan had visualized; despite its promise it did not take the lead in development of an actual university in America.

Henry Tappan's ideas may have been premature for the frontier or it may have been a combination of his personality and habits and of his unique ideas that were unacceptable. At any rate, he was dismissed from the presidency in 1863 and the actual offering of many of the courses that he had added to the curriculum ceased. However, the courses were not removed from the catalog and the foundation remained for the school to later grow on. It did prosper and, as universities developed following the Civil War, it became one of the well-known institutions of higher learning in the country.

VIGNETTE

HENRY PHILLIP TAPPAN (1805-1881)

Tappan was a man of ideas and opinions. He was persuasive but also abrasive, and it was this latter characteristic, along with a personal habit, that got him into trouble at Michigan. The University of Michigan was chartered in 1837 and Tappan became its president in 1852. (Actually, his title was "president and chancellor" and he chose to emphasize the latter because it was similar to titles used in European universities.) He had studied in Prussian and other European universities and had been impressed with the emphases on research and graduate study, and it was his goal to make the "Catholepistemiad" into a place of genius, a university, not just a place to acquire skills to meet the needs of life. These ideas progressed for a time, but when a new board of regents came into power and became opposed to Tappan as a leader he was forced to resign on trumped-up charges (alcoholism — he liked to have a glass of wine with dinner). While he was at Michigan, Tappan continued to pursue his actual first love, a national university to be located in New York City, but this too failed to develop. Tappan had always preferred Europe as a place to live, so he moved back there and remained until his death.

Another pre-Civil War educator whose ideas of higher education were ahead of the time was Philip Lindsley. Lindsley is not as well known as Tappan, perhaps because among the five college presidencies he was offered before finally accepting one he chose Cumberland College in Nashville, Tennessee. Once there, he stuck to that presidency through thick and thin in the face of offers to move to the presidencies of six other institutions and a provostship at Pennsylvania. He graduated from Princeton, did graduate study there, became a tutor and finally vice-president. (Princeton's presidency was among those offered to him.) Lindsley commented on the problems of colleges of his time in speeches made in 1829 and 1837.*

His first comment was that the proliferation of small colleges was the fault of denominations, each of which felt that it must open its own college in each state. The number of prospective students would not allow for all such institutions to be very large. He felt that there was no real justification for this situation in view of the fact that education was intended to be *liberal* and hence universal and not imbued with religious doctrines or beliefs. Lindsley particularly decried the attempts of each small sectarian college to convince people that it was, indeed, liberal in its educational program. He said that it was all right for there to be sectarian colleges, but each should make it clear what beliefs it was teaching.

In Lindsley's view, most colleges should be public, independent of sectarianism, located in large centers of population so that the trustees and faculty would be under surveillance of widely diverse groups. (Of course, he felt that Nashville was a good place for such a college to be located.)

By 1837 many boards of trustees had politicians on them. Lindsley apparently thought that this was good (after all, it would tend to minimize sectarian influences). He did say, however, that if the trustees were affiliated with parties or tried to influence policies along party lines (or to proselyte students to a particular position) this would be a source of alarm. Admitting that there was a spirit of abolitionism in the country (1837 — northern emotions were growing against the "peculiar institution" of slavery in the South) but also

---

*Lindsley, Philip. Baccalaureate Address, Cumberland College, 1829: Commencement Address, 1837. In Richard Hofstadter and Wilson Smith (Eds.): *American Higher Education: A Documentary History*, (Chicago: University of Chicago Press, 1961, vol. I).

spirits of "radicalism, and agrarianism, and ultraism, and amalgamationism, and Loco-Focoism, and Lynchism, and Fanny-Wrightism," he said that the university must prevail in its objectivity. Interestingly, he said that there were those in the country who spoke so strongly in favor of the rights of women that they would abolish family settings with men as the heads in favor of a new system in which women could be equals in such matters.

Lindsley also decried the fact that in the South the professoriat was not respected as it was in the Northeast. He said that being a college trustee in the Northeast was an honor that was sought after. Being a president or professor of a university gave one the biggest and most respectable position attainable in society. And the colleges themselves were respected as seats of learning. It was not this way in Tennessee (and by extension in all of the South). Admitting also that being poor tended to prevent it, Lindsley wanted a literary society for Nashville with the university (Cumberland College — he called it a university) as its centerpiece.

Among the original colonies, New York established a most unique institution in 1784. The state legislature created a corporation called "The Regents of the University of the State of New York." This corporation was given the power to inspect educational institutions and to grant charters and degrees in the state. (Existing corporations, such as Columbia, were excluded.) Thus, the "regents" could found schools and, in effect, the corporation was given the authority usually retained by legislatures. It became a third governing body in the state with respect to education. The "New York Regents" now comprises the entire educational system of New York, since all schools, public and private, have, since its establishment, been incorporated by it and are subject to its visitation. The board consists of 14 persons, elected by the legislature for fourteen-year terms. The board appoints a "President of the University of the State of New York," who thus becomes the state commissioner of education.

Prior to the American Civil War it was clear that the purpose of colleges in this country was to serve the people. Thomas Jefferson, and certainly others as well, wanted them also to serve *learning*. (Tappan's University of Michigan would have been a good example of this; after 1865 the University of Wisconsin under VanHise provided an even more far-reaching example.) Science was probably the primary instrument in causing universities in name to become universities, indeed, centers of learning and research. In 1727 Harvard appointed its first professor of mathematics and natural philosophy. In 1792 Columbia introduced botany to its curriculum, and in 1895 John MacLean became the first professor of chemistry at Princeton. A young student of MacLean's, Benjamin Silliman, became a professor of chemistry and natural history at Yale in 1802; he also studied in Europe and acquired a major collection of minerals and he subsequently taught mineralogy and geology at Yale. In 1818 he founded the *American Journal of Science and Arts*, which spurred the doing and publishing of scientific research in America. Yale became the fountainhead of scientific study in this country. The scientists, in addition to Silliman, were Silliman's son, Benjamin, and his son-in-law, James Dwight Dana at Yale; Amos Eaton, a botanist, and Edward Hitchcock at Amherst (Hitchcock completed the first geological survey for the United States); Ebenezer Emmons at Williams College; and John Torrey and Asa Gray at Harvard. Gray was the recipient of an advance copy of *The Origin of Species* from Darwin in 1859.

The early scientific studies centered on collecting and identifying, but with the establishment of scientific schools (Sheffield Scientific School at Yale, 1847; Lawrence School at Harvard, 1847) science moved more and more toward research. Science gave rise to engineering (although Rensselaer Polytechnic Institute, the first real engineering school, predated these scientific schools). Both science and engineering were in keeping with the spirit of eminent domain that was prevalent in the country.

VIGNETTE

EZRA STILES (1724-1795)

Born in Connecticut to Isaac and Karen Stiles, he attended Yale and graduated in 1736 (age 12) with a license to preach. Later, he studied law at Yale and tutored there

(1749-1755). While at Yale he delivered a particular oration in Latin while Benjamin Franklin happened to be visiting; this so impressed Franklin that the two became lifelong friends. From 1756 he served as the minister of Newport (Rhode Island) Church until it was occupied by British troops in 1777. During this period he was instrumental in the founding of Rhode Island College (Brown). In 1778 he was appointed president of Yale, where he served until his death in 1795. He was a prolific writer, producing 45 volumes of manuscripts. He worked for the abolition of slavery. He founded the American Philosophical Society. Although he was a leading clergyman of the time, Stiles was concerned that a good education should be broader than the religious training then offered in American colleges, and during this presidency Yale moved toward secularization.

All of this occurred in the era of the Yale Report of 1828. This report admitted the need for change to accommodate cultural changes and it applauded the introduction of science and the "spirit of inquiry" into college classes. However, it emphasized the prevalent psychology of the day, faculty psychology, defended lectures and recitations as appropriate learning/teaching procedures, decried secularization through teaching specific professional skills, insisted instead on a classical liberal education to prepare scholars, lamented the lowering of admission standards, and generally defended the old classical curriculum for colleges.

By 1820 the movement toward practical studies in American colleges had gained much momentum; those colleges that retained the classical curriculum (most of the older ones did so) were subject to much criticism and pressure to change. Jeremiah Day was president of Yale at this time. He was a conservative prestigious former professor and had administered the college with care and with success. His conservative attitudes, coupled with the fact that the college was prospering as it was, led him to write the Yale Report of 1828 (with a colleague, Professor James Kingsley, who was a scholar in classics and mathematics). The report was endorsed by a committee of Yale faculty and carried great weight in the academic community until after the Civil War.

The report began with the admission that the curriculum could stand improvement and with the statement that the college intended to make those changes necessary to meet the requirements of the community it served and to aid in the advancement of the country in general. It pointed out that many changes had already been made; chemistry, mineralogy, geology, and other sciences had been added as they grew into mature fields of study; admission requirements had been raised so that the student body was more highly qualified for study; and degree requirements had also been raised.

Asking what was to be the appropriate purpose of a college (specifically of Yale), the report went on to say that it was to lay the foundation for a good education, to provide both breadth and depth of learning in those areas studied, so that the learner could continue his own education. (This was and still is the argument in favor of a liberal education as opposed to a vocational education.) The terminology used in the report said that the purpose of a college education was to provide the *discipline* and the *furniture* of the mind. The discipline reference was clearly to the prevailing notion of the time that the mind operated much as a muscle operates and it needs to be exercised if it is to function well; specifically, the report listed teaching the art of fixing one's attention, of directing a train of thought, of analyzing a subject or a set of information, of following the course of an argument, of balancing evidence, of utilizing one's imagination, and of guiding the thinking process as those mental faculties that should be strengthened through one's education in a college.

In terms of mental furniture, the report defended the subjects being taught by saying that they were intended to provide a balance of character, a more or less standard set of information to be used in the reasoning processes described earlier. Mathematics was intended to illustrate pure reasoning, the physical sciences the process of induction and of dealing with evidence, ancient literature "models of taste," English the power of language in use, logic the art of thinking, rhetoric and oratory the art of speaking. Teaching procedures were also defended in similar terms. Composition exercises were to result in accuracy of expression and declamation was to provide students with extemporaneous reasoning and expression skills. Lectures, if properly presented, were intended to awaken the curiosity of learners and to provide direction for personal study in the textbook.

Recitations, of course, were to assess the learner's progress in his personal study, as well as his depth of understanding.

The tutorial system itself was defended. The report suggested that it was appropriate for each division of study to be headed by a learned professor who would provide instruction in the higher levels of the subject, but it also pointed out that only a few students were at these high levels at any given time while the majority of students were in more beginning phases of knowledge. These beginners could more appropriately be taught by tutors less well versed in the subject than the professor. Furthermore, the use of tutors provided more personal attention for each student, since the learners were assigned in groups to tutors who would stay with them throughout a course.

The report emphasized the fact that Yale's education was not intended to provide graduates with specific professional skills in medicine, theology, law, business, or the mechanical and agricultural arts. Rather, it was intended to provide the basis for students to go on to acquire such skills later. However, it had to admit that there would be those who could not afford to continue their education after the basic college degree was earned. For them it said, "A defective education is better than none." But it added, "A partial education is often expedient; a superficial one, never." The report then asked why all students (those who would go on to professional study and those who would have to be content with a partial course) should take the same set of instruction — in other words, why there should be a single course of study rather than some sort of elective system. The answer was given, again, in terms of faculty psychology. The contents of the courses were said to be not peculiar to any art or profession but necessary as a foundation for all.

The Greek and Roman classics (subjects of particular attack by those who wanted to modernize the curriculum) were defended separately. The major points made were these. A study of these classics lays the foundation for a good taste, since it provides a knowledge upon which to evaluate modern writings. Such a study provides mental discipline at all levels by requiring the learner to follow the original writer's thought processes. The classics provide specific bases for the professions — divinity and law, the proper use and interpretation of language; medicine, familiarity with scientific terminology. The report even went so far as to say that an education based entirely on the classical Greek and Latin literature could in itself be properly regarded as a liberal education.

To the charge that Yale (and other colleges) was not following the pattern of European universities, the report had the following to say. European universities, while good models in general, should not be blindly copied by American institutions because the settings and purposes were vastly different. While European colleges had banded together into universities, the American heritage of individualism had prevented anything like this. Rather, the people had seen fit to establish a multitude of small colleges and not to entrust the development of literature and the arts to fewer large institutions. While this could provide problems of funding, the report said, it also provided for the development of a varied "national literature." Thus, since the purposes were basically different, American colleges ought not copy European universities except slowly and cautiously in those areas of obvious overlap.

Finally, the report spoke to the question of whether or not more American youth ought to be encouraged to participate in college educations, specifically through being provided by the colleges with a more useful final outcome — a vocation or at least some of the skills that would lead to a vocation. (Merchants, manufacturers, and farmers were specifically listed as those groups concerned.) The argument, again, was based on faculty psychology, saying that whatever the working status or profession of an individual, what was needed when he became engaged in making public decisions was the same liberal education that had been defended earlier. As to the question of whether it would not be advisable for more of the "working classes" to be admitted to college, the point was made that this would be desirable *but* could not be accomplished at the expense of lowering the admission requirements, since this would have the long-term effect of lowering the level of the college education itself. Instead, the report suggested that one of the major changes needed at Yale was a raising of admission standards.

In college curricula as well as in the general language of the day, "science" prior to 1859 meant any well-organized statement of principles in any area of knowledge. The key criteria were order, systematic procedures, and an understood regularity in statements of information and rules. This "science" also was essentially deductive, not empirical, although the purpose was to establish principles of operation or behavior (laws in the common terminology) by which one could predict future events. There was, however, a tendency to associate "science" with natural phenomena. Thus, there were *natural history* and *natural philosophy* in curricula of early colleges.

The modern professor in a university, if asked what it is that makes a given institution a true university, would probably say that it is its contribution to knowledge. The Johns Hopkins was a university primarily because it offered opportunities for advanced study beyond the levels of existing colleges, but it also offered this opportunity to its teachers — that is, they could do research. The new University of Chicago was successful in attracting eminent scholars because William Rainey Harper not only said that research was important in a university but also backed this up by (a) continuing his own scholarship even as president and (b) rewarding those professors who were able to do research and to publish the results with academic honors (higher salaries, promotions, tenure). Research in the modern sense, however, is a relatively new thing in academe. It can be truly said that it began with publication of *The Origin of Species* in 1859.

In the early post-Darwin era (actually the post-*Origin of Species* era), science came to be associated closely with the collection of data, with the obtaining of evidence related to material or natural phenomena. The Darwinian suggestions were based on careful accumulation of data and upon analysis of this data; they were so "radical" that they made a solid impression upon academics, not only in terms of their content but also in terms of how they were arrived at. In this era natural history and natural philosophy gave way to *science* (or sciences) in college curricula. Still later, emphasis came to be placed on the processes of science — identification of a problem, accumulation of information, statement of hypotheses, testing of hypotheses, replication of tests, generalization or stating of principles — and it was seen that these might be applicable to any content, even to man and his institutions. Basically, science questioned beliefs and subjected them to investigation (data collection and hypothesis testing). The major meaning of "science" for a time was blurred by its application to such a wide variety of subject areas. However, this has turned around again to a considerable extent, so that today "science" usually means one of the theoretical areas that have to do with natural or material phenomena (chemistry, biology, physics, astronomy, geology and the like), and people are at least a bit uncomfortable when they hear of "political science" or "social science." (Since these terms are still used what has happened is that many people sort of subconsciously say to themselves when these terms are used, "Oh, they mean that scientific procedures are used in the study." Thus, they place the non-natural "sciences" into a different category from the "true sciences.")

The growth of modern science following Darwin's work was phenomenal. It was not so much the content of *The Origin of Species* but the ideas it engendered that led to this growth. First of all, it became clear that a way of acquiring new knowledge was to make careful observations, to obtain empirical data, and then to generalize on these observations; this was Darwin's actual contribution. But second, it also became clear that existing beliefs could be called into question; after all, if Darwin could question a biblical belief surely any man-made belief could be so questioned. (In truth, there was no need to feel that the biblical belief had been questioned as I will show a bit later, but nevertheless many people at the time felt that this was the case.) Third, there grew along with the developing sciences the experimental methods that involved controlling variables while making observation so that cause-and-effect relationships could be established (or, more correctly, inferred), and that also involved theorizing and the testing of theories by observation, whether controlled or not.

Now, this did not all develop at once; the process was, itself, evolutionary. At first (following Darwin) the idea was that science consisted of observational verification, whether it was a principle or a theory that was to be verified. Science was solid, physical, and sort of like a puzzle in which there were lots of missing pieces. But the pieces were "out there somewhere" waiting to be found, and when they were found they would be seen to fit neatly into the developing picture of our world. As mathematics also grew, primarily as a tool of science, its abstractness led scientists to recognize that there was (or could be) much abstractness in science also. One could speculate or invent ideas out of pure thought and use these ideas, theories, in trying to explain cause and effect among natural phenomena. And once an explanation had been invented, the inventor could set up experiments to test it to try to determine the extent to which it would work or not work in other situations.

Thus, science and its methodology grew from inductive accumulation of information with the resulting stating of regularities, principles, through empirical examination of questions using controlled situations to try to discover cause-effect relationships, to theoretical experimentation in which an explanation was invented and then examined experimentally. As these procedures developed in the sciences they were also applied in other fields with the resulting large growth of knowledge in those fields as well. However, there is some doubt that it was totally wise to apply the methods of science, related to physical phenomena where caprice does not operate, in those areas of study that involve human beings, where caprice (or mind if you prefer) does operate. Thus, scientific methods may be very useful in certain studies in psychology, but other methods may have to be modified to fit other situations). We may now be in this advanced state of research in which scientific methods are not *the* epitome but are only a basis from which all research can continue to grow. If so, our modern universities can become even greater pillars of learning than the great institutions of the past.

The scientific disciplines are true theoretical disciplines; within them progress is made by theorizing (making speculative explanations) and testing theories. Many other disciplines claim to be theory-based, but it is doubtful that in any of them the nature of the theories is as precise as it is in the sciences.*

Laws and theories are fundamentally different parts of the collection of information and speculation that is science; specifically, laws are part of the information of science while theories are part of the speculation of science and the two should not be intermingled (even though they have been intermingled in the past, occasionally, when we didn't know any better). There is a myth among scientists, or at least among some groups of us, that "hypothesis" is a step in a progression that begins with information or data and ends with a law

---

*See Westmeyer, Paul, "The Nature of Disciplines." *Journal of Research in Science Teaching,* March 1983, Vol. 20, No. 3, pp. 265-270. Material related to this same topic, the nature of *scientific* disciplines, is given in several pages here following.

and that "theory" precedes "law." The progression is information, hypothesis, theory, law. As I said, this is a myth. Actually, an hypothesis may precede either a theory or a law, but it may also precede individual pieces of information (as I intend to show) and a true theory can never become a law.

The body of knowledge in science, as I hinted above, consists of two parts, information and speculation. Progress in science involves accumulating information, looking for and stating regularities among isolated pieces of information so that predictions can be made of future events, deliberately searching for answers to questions that are of concern to us, and speculating on possible explanations regarding the causes of phenomena. This is true of chemistry and of all the other natural sciences; it is also true of the social sciences, except that there may be less emphasis on speculation regarding cause and effect and more emphasis on the other three processes, especially on the finding of regularities among isolated bits of information. In the natural sciences we are fortunate that the subjects of our investigation (except in the life sciences) have no wills of their own and are subject to the regulation of forces that can be discovered and measured. To the extent that capricious behavior is possible among the subjects of an investigation, the information that comes out of that investigation will be suspect; if capricious behavior is not possible, the information from an investigation can be taken as factual. It is safe; to assume that the actions of chemicals are not capricious; thus, when information is discovered regarding the behavior of a given chemical this can be taken as factual and used from that time forward. The same is true of the behavior of objects investigated by physicists, of astronomical bodies, of rocks and minerals, and of all other inanimate objects and materials. It is also true of those aspects of behavior among animate objects and materials that are subject only to *forces* and not in any way controlled by a *will*. (There is, of course, a problem with precisely determining when *will* has a bearing on actions in living materials. As a matter of fact it is pretty hard even to define *will*. We might simply think of *will* as any factor that can have an effect on behavior besides those things which we call physical, including electrical, forces. Of course, we must also realize that we have invented the idea of forces even though we can measure them. *Forces* are then more "real" than *will* simply because we can measure them.)

Chemists are interested in the characteristics of initial and final states of systems, for knowing these enables us to say what substances will result from combinations, recombinations, or disintegrations of other substances. Chemists are also interested in what has to be done to bring about changes from an initial state to a final state in a system. (This is a matter of practical interest, since the knowledge can enable us to set up producing systems to yield desired materials.) Studying initial and final states of systems and determining what must be done to effect the change is frequently not as simple as it sounds, but, in any event, this kind of investigation leads to factual information, information that cannot be disputed. Reactants and products can be identified, contained, and measured. I could mix a weighed amount of powdered KI with a weighed amount of powdered $Pb(NO^3)^2$ in a beaker. This contained system, then, could be considered an initial state. Then I could add water and stir the mixture thoroughly until equilibrium is reached — until no more white powder remains and no more yellow precipitate is being formed. Then I could analyze this final state and identify what is present and determine the quantities of each material. Of course, I also know what had to be done to bring about the change from the initial state to the final state; I added water and stirred the mixture. I realize that this is a very simple example, but I am suggesting this as an illustration of the point that the knowledge obtained from this kind of experimentation is factual knowledge. It was just such factual knowledge, accumulated over a period of time, that led to the stating of the law of combining proportions.

Correct observations of non-capricious behaviors produce factual information; observations of possible capricious behavior may also produce factual information, but the observer has to be very careful regarding what is stated as the observation. (To say that a paramecium moves away from the spot where acetic acid was injected into its environment may be a factual observation; to say that the paramecium moved from a region of low pH to one of higher pH would be stretching factuality; to say that the paramecium was irritated by the acetic acid would be stating a very questionable observation.) The accumulation of factual information certainly represents progress in science. However, scientists are not content with such mere accumulation; instead they look for regularities among pieces of information — they try to relate events to one another by some formula or statement of principle and when they think they have found such a statement it is proposed as a tentative law, more precisely at this point, as an hypothesis. (*Hypothesis* has several connotations; in the present use it is a preliminary statement of a regularity that, hopefully, can be stated as a law after it has been checked out. The law of combining proportions was an hypothesis when first stated; then after it had been examined in several additional systems and found to hold true it was stated as a law — an observed regularity among data.) A law, then, is just a restatement of a set of facts; it has the advantage that the regularity which it describes may be expected to be applicable to many other situations besides those initially observed. The law of combining proportions has proven to be extremely useful; so have the gas laws and many others, not only in chemistry but also in the other sciences.

A law, being a generalization, is subject to verification. All one has to do is to set up a new set of conditions and see if what the law predicts does indeed happen. If I observe that potatoes boiled in an open pot at sea level get well done in 20 minutes and that they get less and less well done in the same time interval if they are boiled at locations higher and higher above sea level, I can state a law of boiling potatoes that says, "Potatoes get less and less well done if boiled for equal periods of time at locations of increasing altitude." Then I would predict that going to a location below sea level, for example, would cause the potatoes to get beyond well done in 20 minutes when boiled in an open container or that going to a still higher location than those used to establish the law in the first place would result in even less well-done potatoes. To test my law, I just have to go to the locations specified and see if what I expect to happen does indeed happen.

Laws, then, are based on observation; they are generalizations and they are subject to testing on the basis of their predictions. As I said earlier, a law may have grown out of an hypothesis. A scientist who has in hand a set of observations may make a guess regarding a commonality among them; he may then predict what would happen in a new situation if the hypothesis is correct, and he can set up an experiment to see if what he predicted does happen. In this way a sort of preliminary law (an hypothesis) may be made into a law.

A second way in which science progresses is through deliberately seeking answers to important questions. A chemist has a question that needs to be answered; he devises possible ways to find an answer and continues to pursue them until he either finds an answer or gives up. (One of the earliest treatments for venereal disease carried the number 606 because it was the six hundred and sixth material that researchers had tried.) No doubt the bulk of scientific research today follows this mode of making progress. I analyzed the titles of papers presented at the 1982 meeting of the Texas Academy of Science, for example, and found that there were 115 descriptive papers, 12 on historical topics, 21 reporting correlational findings, 17 reporting studies that apparently involved experimental manipulation of one or more variables to try to determine cause-and-effect relationships, and 12 reporting studies that could have involved theory verification. All of these except for the final 12 would appear to have their base in the search for answers to specific questions (unless some of the 115 in the first category were just random information seeking, which I doubt).

The stating of hypotheses also has a place in this second mode of progress in science. What I called above "devising possible ways to find an answer" really means making a guess either as to what the answer is or as to where it might be found, and either of these is hypothesizing. Earlier I said that an *hypothesis* was a preliminary statement of a regularity among data; here it is a guess (presumably an educated guess based on some preliminary information) regarding the answer to a specific question. Here, as earlier, the reason for stating an hypothesis is to have a place to start, something to check out by experiment, a guide to further searches for information. Hypotheses are for testing and, if not found to be incorrect, they may lead to the statement of a law or to the answer to a specific question.

The third mode of progress in science is the one we like to think of as our major procedure, but it isn't our major procedure at all, as I suggested above. This is theorizing or speculating on the explanations for observed phenomena. A theory is an attempt to explain observations when they cannot be explained by citing facts. It may be an answer to the question, why? Why do objects thrown into the air fall to earth? Why do gases behave as they do in confined volumes? Why do substances exhibit the characteristics that they do? Why do chemicals combine to produce new substances with characteristics different from those of the original materials? Or it may answer the question, how did this come about (which is a kind of "why" question)? How did such a variety of bird species occur? How did the planets get where they are? How did the reactions in our sun get started?

The atomic theory was an attempt to explain why substances behave as they do, particularly why they combine and disintegrate in chemical reactions. The many modifications of the basic atomic theory which we are still experiencing are attempts to make the explanation more inclusive (so that it can be used to make a broader range of explanations for behaviors) and more "correct" (so that parts of earlier theories that have been found to be no longer useful have been replaced with ideas that work better). The theory of relativity was an attempt to interrelate, and so to explain, the phenomena associated with exchanges of energy and between matter and energy, including the "violation" of the law of conservation of mass that suggests that at velocities near the speed of light moving objects undergo changes in mass. The theory of evolution was an attempt to explain, by interrelating phenomena, the apparent similarities among many species — indeed, it was an attempt to explain speciation itself. Several different theories have been proposed to explain the origin of the universe and the solar system in which we live. The ideas of force (mentioned earlier) and energy constitute a theory, although we may not call it a theory, that attempts to explain a large variety of phenomena — from the fact that the parts of an atom stick together but can be separated to the fact that the solar planets follow observable orbits.

So, to recapitulate, we have three procedures through which science progresses: (1) the accumulation of factual information, along with the statement of laws which describe regularities among facts, (2) the deliberate seeking of answers to specific questions, which results in additional accumulation of factual information and which, presumably, could also result in the stating of additional laws if there were detected regularities among the facts, and (3) speculation or the stating of theories which can serve to explain behaviors of things, substances, or organisms. These are not mutually exclusive and, indeed, may frequently be interrelated. Oftentimes, a theory will suggest a way to proceed in attempting to find an answer to a question, for example. "Checking out" a law by applying it in new situations may result in the discovery of new facts that the law doesn't fit. Similarly, when a theory is applied to a new situation it may fail to explain observations adequately. The results of these last two situations are different, as I'll explain shortly.

As I said earlier, as accumulation of facts may lead to the statement of an hypothesis and eventually to the statement of a law. A scientific law is the statement of a generalization from limited but extensive facts to what may be expected in all future cases. If 5,000 tennis balls thrown into the air fall back to earth, it can probably be predicted that ball 5,001 thrown into the air will also fall to earth. If everything thrown into the air falls back to earth over a period of observations, it may be safe to generalize that anything thrown into the air in the future will also fall to earth. Indeed, one may state a *law* regarding the falling to earth of objects thrown into the air. Of course, this law would have been true for objects thrown into the air by man until fairly recently, wouldn't it? But it isn't completely true anymore — since we have become able to send objects into space permanently.

Can a law be undone by findings which are counter to the predictions of the law? Now that we have been able to throw things into the air which did not fall back to earth, must we give up the law of falling objects? Now that we have found that in certain specific reactions the thing we call mass either increases or decreases, must we give up the law of conservation of mass? No, we do not give up a law, once it has been stated. After all, a generalization that grew out of a large number of observations (facts) can't be wrong. We may limit the applicability of the law; this is what was done in the two cases just cited. Or we may expand the law to take into account the cases that it failed to predict. Each of Boyle's and Charles's gas laws is limited because it holds a variable constant; each is expanded by adding the other so that we have the combined gas law (which, incidentally, is still limited in its applicability). Universal gravitation is, of course, an extension of earth gravitation. A law is, indeed, "proven" when its predictions turn out to be correct — proven in the sense that it has been demonstrated that it applies in the new situations as well as in the original ones.

Can a theory be undone by findings which it fails to explain? If atomic theory fails to explain behaviors of substances in cases where it ought to do so, will we give it up in favor of some replacement? If the types of force and energy that we have invented fail to explain some new observations, will we either give up the old ideas or invent new ones, or both? If factual information is found that does not fit in with the theory of evolution, will we give up the theory?

In revisions of the atomic theory, we have come to a very complex system of forces, radiation quanta, and matter quanta, in addition to the ideas of particles that most of us are more familiar with (protons, electrons, and neutrons). The problem was that our theory was not adequate to explain certain facts, so new ideas were invented that would explain them. Gravitational and electromagnetic forces were not enough to explain nuclear bonding, so "strong" forces were invented, and along with them "weak" forces. These led to the ideas of quarks, leptons, and neutrinos, etc. Very elaborate systems of investigation have been devised to test the unified picture of the behavior of matter that has resulted, the basis being attempts to find evidence regarding the decay of protons. When such evidence is found, will this have proven the correctness of the quantum field theory? It certainly will not. Each of the earlier theories that we used was tested and verified as being "correct" in its time. Yet each has been modified, if not discarded entirely, by the finding of new phenomena that the theory failed to explain adequately. (Think of the "plum pudding" model, for example, or the simple orbiting electron model for atoms. Each was correct for its time, but neither is very useful now — they have been replaced.)

As scientists we create problems for ourselves, but more importantly for our public, when we speak of theories as if they were on the same plane as observations. They are, in fact, on both a much higher plane and a much lower plane. They are far above mere facts in that they are useful for making interconnections among facts and predicting future events (facts, observations). They are far below observations in that they are only the inventions of clever minds and are not real. As scientists we sometimes get so caught up in our ideas that we fail to remember the simple homily of Thomas Huxley — "The great tragedy of science — the slaying of a beautiful theory by an ugly fact." In other words, we come to believe that our theories are true and sometimes we even try to convince others that this is the case when all that we really ought to be doing is using the theories as long as they turn out to be applicable and then seeking ways to modify or replace them. We ought to have no "pride of ownership" in a theory just because it resides in our discipline, science. Rather, we ought to have a "pride of change" in that we should be constantly on the lookout for the inapplicability of theories so that we can change them.

As I said, earlier, theories are also not on the same plane as laws. However, there has been some confusion of these two terms — if not of the two constructs. The Ptolemaic "theory" was an attempt to explain the movements of bodies with reference to each other, and it was eventually replaced with the Copernican "theory." The phlogiston "theory" was an attempt to explain certain behaviors of substances and it was eventually replaced by the oxygen "theory." However, we don't think of the last of these as the oxygen *theory* anymore. Neither do we think of the behaviors of heavenly bodies in terms of Copernican *theory*; we have been able to make observations so that we can know what is out there (within limits) and how objects are relatively placed. We have been able to send rockets to distant objects and we can know from observations how these objects move with respect to each other. Wouldn't it be better to say that the Copernican *hypothesis* has not been found inapplicable and so we can state a law regarding the positioning and movements of heavenly objects? Wouldn't it also be better to say that the oxygen *hypothesis* has been found to work out well and so we can state a law regarding the behavior of certain chemicals in terms of oxygen as a component of the systems? Hypotheses can be wrong; if they are we just give them up and perhaps state replacement hypotheses. Is it possible that with respect to our solar system we will find the Copernican hypothesis to be wrong? Is it possible that someone will prove that oxygen does not exist or that it doesn't combine with other substances? Neither of these is likely to happen, so we can take the step that makes them laws in these cases.

If there were theories in the past that ought not have been called theories, are there laws that are improperly so called? Is the conservation of energy a law? Well, the statement certainly describes a regularity among observations, but the problem is that the construct that is being used is just that — a construct, an invention. We can observe temperatures and temperature changes but only by observing the presumed effect of what we call temperature on a column of mercury or a metal thermocouple or a substance electrically sensitive to temperature changes. We can observe the presence of electrical energy by using appropriate devices (light bulbs, meters) and we can measure the presumed expenditure of other types of energy by their effects, such as the dent made by a falling object or the fact that one moving object that collides with another can change the motion of the second object. But the fact among all of this is that energy was invented to be conserved. Energy was to explain the interconnections among phenomena, such as the compositional changes in a battery and the glowing of a light bulb attached to the battery, or the fact that certain chemical systems must be heated to undergo a change while other systems give up heat while changing spontaneously (heat being our invention to relate such changes to temperature). Since energy would be useful only if it did not behave capriciously, the law of conservation of energy was necessary as a part of the invention. This, then, is not a law at all; it is part of a theory even though we are accustomed to calling it the law of conservation of energy.

Let's try to tie all of this together. Science information consists of facts and speculations. Facts result from observations of situations in which capricious behavior is presumed not to be possible and, cautiously, of other situations as well. Laws are stated as outlines of regularities among observed facts, each law having been preceded for some length of time and for some period of testing by an hypothesis. Hypotheses may also be stated preceding the search for answers to specific questions. Theories, on the other hand, are speculative in nature. They are invented for the purpose of explaining observations or laws and they utilize ideas rather than citing other factual information. While a law can be proven, even though its applicability may have to be limited, a theory cannot be proven because it does not utilize facts but ideas. An hypothesis normally also precedes the statement of a theory. In this case the purpose of the hypothesis is a sort of trial of the preliminary ideas before a formal statement is made of the theory. Any of the hypotheses described may be found to be incorrect or inapplicable; in this event the hypothesis is simply modified or discarded. However, once a law or a theory has been formulated (after testing, as described, through hypotheses), the law remains a part of our information while the theory may remain, be modified eventually, or be replaced entirely when it is found to be no longer useful.

If we were actually as precise as we like to think we are in science, we would limit our theories to those situations that are governed by an uncertainty principle. The three uncertainty principles are: (a) the Heisenberg uncertainty principle, (b) the statement that historical data cannot provide dynamic information, and (c) the statement that an entity that can be measured only by observing effects of which the entity is the presumed cause cannot be demonstrated to exist. This would ensure that what we call theories are, indeed, in the realm of speculation, and it would lay to rest the notion that a theory can somehow become a law if we just give it enough time and test it thoroughly enough. Under this precision, clearly our atomic theories would remain theories because of principle (a), the theory of evolution and the theories regarding origins of universes and heavenly bodies would remain theories because of principle (b), and force and energy would remain theory because of principle (c). I suggest that, in general, we *are* about as precise as I have said we should be. Our major theories are, indeed, explanations that are recognized as limited by one or more uncertainly principles. Perhaps we could be more careful in referring to lesser explanations (not limited by an uncertainly principle) as *hypotheses* rather than theories.

It is this "nature of scientific theories" that limits the applicability of the so-called scientific method of research in non-science fields. It is also this information that caused me to say earlier that the biblical beliefs in the time of Darwin did not need to be questioned; evolution was (and is) a theory in the truest sense of the word as just explained. Nevertheless, it was Darwin who sparked the scientific revolution and the research revolution in American higher education.

Henry Phillip Tappan's idea of a university was most prominently expounded in connection with the proposal for a national university to be located in New York City. Even while he was president at Michigan and attempting to make that school into a university, he was also continuing his efforts to found a university in New York. In New York, the Astor Library was acquiring a reputation as a seat of learning. The sciences were growing in stature and Tappan had a scientist son-in-law. In New York, Peter Cooper was indicating a willingness to donate large sums of money for higher education. Tappan put these together into a proposal for an institution to be called the University and Academy of Sciences and Arts of the City of New York. This institution was to serve as the capstone of the educational system, with the colleges beneath it in the hierarchy preparing men to enter the university for advanced work. It was to employ professors who could gather learned men around themselves and teach at a high level as well as do research.

Tappan tried to obtain funds from Cooper, Astor, other donors of smaller amounts, and the city itself for his university. Cooper was interested in supplying funds for a scientific building, the Astor library was already there as mentioned, and private funds could provide additional structures; public funds, then, could go toward operation of the school. Cooper had an additional idea which was to rent parts of his building to the city (or anyone who could use it) and to use the rent money for operating funds. He wanted to call this operation a "union." Among the names for whatever new institution was to develop were "Cooper Scientific Institute," "Cooper University," and the earlier one "University and Academy." Remember that the initial idea was to make this into a national university (*the* national university).

Things sort of fell apart, mostly due to the fact that public funds were not appropriated as hoped. Also, Peter Cooper apparently had his own fixed ideas. He did construct his "union" and it began operation in 1859. He remained interested in incorporating it with other units into a university, offering to do so, eventually, with Columbia. However, this incorporation never came about and the national university idea once more failed to bear fruit.

By the mid 1800s America was becoming two rather distinct "countries," even three if the frontier were to be thought of separately. James Dwight Dana urged Yale to expand itself into the American University in 1856, and, as we have seen, there had been other moves toward a university at one place or another in the country — in the North. But in the South there was (1) a lack of confidence in the permance of the union and (2) a lack of confidence in its own colleges. A central University of the South was proposed in 1857 in a publication called *DeBow's Review*.* The argument was first that existing institutions were not sufficiently "Southern" nor sufficiently central to serve the whole region. And, in addition, there were too few institutions to which southern boys could go for an appropriate education. The second argument was that there was need for a centralized institution to proclaim the doctrines espoused by the South and to counteract the teachings of northern doctrines to which too many southern youth were being exposed. Third, the southern institutions had low standards and their degrees were superficial; there was a need to upgrade southern education in general and this could best be accomplished through a single institution supported by the whole South.

In 1856 Bishop Leonidas Polk of Louisiana sent a letter to his fellow Episcopal bishops in North Carolina, South Carolina, Georgia, Florida, Tennessee, Alabama, Mississippi, Arkansas, and Texas suggesting that these nine dioceses cooperate with him in establishing a southern university. Bishop Polk apparently saw both a threat in the northern educational systems which then provided most of the education for southern clergy and a promise of Christian liberal education for southern youth in the proposed southern institution. He also saw that the existing southern colleges were, as mentioned above, relatively low level and not at all comparable with European universities. Thus, he actually envisioned a southern university to which the students who graduated from existing colleges would come for advanced training and study.

At the General Convention of the Episcopal Church in 1856 a resolution was passed by the southern bishops to begin such a university as described. Articles of organization were drawn up and approved in the ten dioceses and a board of trustees was set up. (The

*Information in this section taken from Storr, Richard, J., *The Beginnings of Graduate Education in America*. (New York: Arno Press, 1969.)

board consisted of the bishop of each diocese, one other clergyman from each, and two laymen from each diocese. This board met in July of 1857 at Lookout Mountain, Tennessee, and began the actual planning of the university. It was at this meeting that the way was paved for fund raising; two of the bishops, including Polk, were appointed to head this effort. The effort was based on the idea that the new institution should not be a sectarian one but rather a true southern university, a literary center, a seat of learning and research, and a leader in elevating the minds and so the culture of the South. The trustees had agreed that the actual construction of the university would not begin until pledges of $500,000 had been amassed. This was accomplished rather quickly and so the planning proceeded. The university was to be set up in colleges (32 of them but each roughly equivalent to a modern-day department). There was to be a master's degree program, as well as the bachelor's. And following completion of a master's degree, a student could become a resident fellow for both further study and teaching.

The university buildings were planned for construction at Sewanee, Tennessee, and the first cornerstone was laid on October 9, 1860. At the ceremony there were over 5,000 people, and one of the principal speakers was Frederick A.P. Barnard, president of the University of Mississippi. Barnard had become a believer in the need for graduate-level studies and he had proposed such a program for his university. His speech at Sewanee so impressed the trustees, especially Polk and Green (Bishop of Mississippi), that he was offered the presidency of the University of the South. But for the Civil War the South might have produced an actual graduate school in this new institution. However, the buildings were burned along with all of the school's records. Bishop Polk served as a general in the southern army and was killed in action. And in 1864 Frederick A.P. Barnard moved to Columbia as its president.

Following the Civil War, the University of the South was rebuilt and began awarding degrees in 1873. By that time, of course, the South was no longer a really separate entity and, besides this, other institutions developed in southern regions that were to take a lead in the evolution of higher education. The University of the South has remained a small school.

VIGNETTE

FREDERICK AGUSTUS PORTER BARNARD (1809-1889)

Barnard College (founded in 1889, the year of Barnard's death) is named after F.A.P. Barnard and is a monument to his inability to establish coeducation at Columbia. Barnard was educated at Yale and taught in a grammar school in his early career. Eventually, however, he returned to his alma mater as a professor. He was appointed to the presidency of the University of Mississippi in 1856 and remained there until 1860 when he was chosen as the first president of the University of the South. (As noted in the text, he had made a favorable impression in a dedicatory speech at that institution.) Development of the University of the South, however, was interrupted by the Civil War and Barnard became president of Columbia. At Columbia Barnard established a pattern that was to be emulated later by William Rainey Harper at Chicago. He separated the first two years of study from the last two. The freshman and sophomore years were to be devoted to those things that "trained the mind" a la the popular faculty psychology of the day and the junior and senior years were to be devoted to scholarly study. Barnard also felt strongly that women should receive an education in the same institution as men and he pushed for coeducational programs at Columbia. He was successful only in getting a separate-but-equal institution for women, an annex to the university, Barnard College.

Another proposal of the pre-Civil War years did not bear fruit. A national university had been proposed by Benjamin Rush in 1788. His would have been a utilitarian school, de-emphasizing classical education and emphasizing education for daily needs and job skills. George Washington left money in his will to begin such an institution and his five immediate successors in the presidency supported the idea. Congress, in committee, endorsed the idea in 1816, but the nearest the university actually came to being was when John Smithson (a British scientist) left a bequest to the United States government for the establishment of "a learned institution" in Washington; this was in 1835. Francis Wayland, president of Brown, urged a school for intellectuals who had completed liberal arts studies — a university, once more. However, Congress used the money to establish quite a different kind of "learned institution" — one nonetheless important or useful to the nation but, nevertheless, completely unlike a university. The Federal University never got off the ground.

VIGNETTE

JAMES MADISON (1750 or 51-1836)

> Schooled at the College of New Jersey, Madison was Jefferson's secretary of state and, of course, he later became president of the United States. In this office (in 1810) he proposed a national university. He was a Unitarian and believed, as did Jefferson, in complete separation of church and state; hence, he believed that a secular institution was badly needed in the country. He approached Congress with the idea that the university could be built with funds obtained by selling unused federal land in the District of Columbia. A committee of Congress decided that it would not be constitutional to support such a school with public funds. After an interlude occasioned by the War of 1812, Madison again recommended founding of a national university in 1815. This time, however, he failed to send along an itemized budget for support of the proposed school and the matter was tabled by Congress. In 1816 he tried a third time and this time the House approved but the Senate did not. (It was said by Timothy Dwight of Yale that the real reason for the failure of Congress to act favorably on the national university was pressure from religious groups which did not want to see a publicly supported secular institution founded.)

As I said earlier, the *Dartmouth College* case apparently opened the door to the founding of many small colleges in America. This college-opening spirit lasted right up until the Civil War and was particularly prominent just before that war (more than twice as many colleges were founded between 1850 and 1860 than had been founded in the previous ten-year period. Of course, most of the institutions were small (very small), sometimes a college had a building but no students, sometimes it had a building but no professor, sometimes only professors and nothing else, and on occasion a president but no teachers. Funding was always a problem.

Professors at South Carolina were paid $1,500 per year in the early 1800s and the same was true at Virginia in 1820. Harvard paid $2,000 by 1830 and doubled this salary by 1860, but by far a more likely salary for a college professor in the pre-Civil War period was $600-$800 per year.

Illinois College had nine students at its opening in 1829. Emory College (Atlanta, Georgia) opened on the *promise* of interest not yet earned on subscriptions not yet collected. The first graduation class of the University of Michigan consisted of eleven students.

Nassau Hall at Princeton burned during this period. The first building at Ohio College (Athens, Ohio) was struck by lightening; Maine Hall at Bowdoin burned. The main building at Vermont burned and the college nearly failed as a result of this disaster. Half of the University of Georgia burned.

On the positive side, many of the new colleges of this period included science in the curriculum in some way. Also, many of the established institutions added scientific schools. Harvard added the Lawrence Scientific School in 1847 and Yale added the Sheffield School in the same year. Dartmouth started the Chandler School of Science and Arts in 1851. Some of the now-prominent scientific schools also began in this era. Rensselaer Polytechnic Institute was established in 1824, considerably before the rise of science in other schools. The Polytechnic Institute of Brooklyn was founded in 1854 and Massachusetts Institute of Technology began in 1861.

So what was the fate of the 800 colleges founded between 1776 and 1861? Some illustrative fates in selected states:

Arkansas (3 colleges)   100% mortality

Florida (2)	100% mortality
Kansas (20)	95% mortality
Texas (40)	95% mortality—only two survived, Baylor and Austin College
Missouri (85 colleges and so the worst total mortality record)	90% (8 survivors)
Pennsylvania (31 colleges, best survival record)	48% (16 survivors)

Meanwhile, a congressman from Vermont, Justin Smith Morrill, suggested in 1848 that American colleges might well "lop off a portion of the studies established centuries ago as the mark of European scholarship and replace the vacancy — if it is a vacancy — by those of a less antique and more practical value." What he had in mind was a technical kind of education which would include agriculture, the major business of the United States. Pennsylvania had a Farmer's High School in 1854 and later it became the Agriculture College of Pennsylvania in 1862. The New York State Agricultural College opened in 1860. The West, although primarily agricultural, was not very scientifically interested and had only one comparable school, the Michigan State College of Agriculture at East Lansing (1857). The Morrill Act was first introduced in Congress in 1857 and it passed — amidst opposition. The South opposed it because it was seen as a strengthening of the artisan and laboring classes of the North; the West opposed it because they wanted "no fancy farmers and no fancy mechanics." President Buchanan vetoed the bill. However, it was resubmitted in 1862, passed Congress, and was signed into law by President Lincoln. This bill actually began a new era of higher education in America. Cornell University, founded with the aid of land grant funds, was to take a prominent lead in the development of university education.

On April 12, 1861 units of the growing military forces of the South (it wasn't actually a confederacy at this time) fired on Fort Sumter in Charleston (South Carolina) harbor.

CHAPTER 3

MOVEMENT TOWARD A TRUE UNIVERSITY

The Morrill Act of 1862 provided:

1. support in every state for at least one college devoted to agriculture and the mechanic arts,
2. public lands or land script equal to 30,000 acres for each senator and representative under the 1860 apportionment (a total of 17,430,000 acres of public land),
3. the funds, except for 10 percent which could be used initially to buy land for sites, to be set up as an endowment at no less than 5 percent interest,
4. if not used the funds to be returned to the federal government in five years.

PUBLIC lands sold under the program reached the highest price in New York at $6.73 per acre, the lowest in Rhode Island at $0.41 per acre, and the average price was $1.65. In reality, not a whole lot of funding was available for the A & M's, but they did develop.

Actually as early as 1787 the Ohio Company had obtained a grant of two townships for the support of a university, the first "federal" land grant (under the Articles of Confederation) for higher education. Afterward, every new state west of the Appalachians was also granted funds for support of a university. The money generally provided only an opening, however, and the states had to appropriate operating funds; the frontier anti-intellectualism generally tended to prevent this, along with the continuing sectarian objections to public, secular education.

61

Cornell University was founded in 1865. The Second Morrill Act was passed in 1890; this provided for regular, annual federal appropriations for land-grant colleges (and, incidentally, began the "separate but equal" facilities for Negroes in 17 states). The land-grant institutions were set up as follows:

- Michigan, Pennsylvania, Maryland, and Iowa created A & M's out of previously chartered agricultural colleges.
- Wisconsin, Minnesota, North Carolina, and Missouri turned the grants over to existing state universities to set up the new programs.
- Oklahoma, South Dakota, and Washington set up new A & M colleges in competition with existing state universities.
- Ohio, California, Arkansas, and West Virginia founded new state universities and added A & M components.

Six states arranged for existing private colleges to provide the A & M education: Connecticut in the Sheffield Scientific School of Yale, Rhode Island in Brown University, New Hampshire in Dartmouth College, New Jersey in Rutgers, Kentucky in Transylvania College (founded as a seminary in 1783), and Oregon in Methodist College of Corvallis (now Oregon State).

In other states:

- Delaware revived Delaware College.
- Massachusetts opened a new A & M but put part of the funds into MIT also.
- Indiana used its land grant funds plus private funds to found Purdue University (named after the donor of $100,000, John Purdue).
- New York, like Indiana, used land-grant funds with private funds ($500,000 donated by John Cornell) to found Cornell University.
- Texas requires a longer story and that story follows in the form of excerpts from an unpublished paper written by a student in one of my graduate classes.*

When the federal government was established under the Con-

---

*Padgett, Claude. "The Permanent University Fund: A Fund for Excellence." Paper submitted in HED 5003, UTSA, Nov. 1980.

stitution of 1789, the United States became the sole proprietor of the public lands and held title to all such lands acquired under the Treaty of 1783. In addition, various states ceded lands to the federal government when they joined the union. Texas, however, developed under a foreign government and became a state through annexation. It retained control of its own public lands. When the Republic of Texas was founded in 1836, it laid claim to vast areas of land — some 216,314,560 acres. (Of course, it did not actually retain all of this land because some of it was in New Mexico, Kansas, Colorado, Wyoming, and Oklahoma.) In 1838 President Mirabeau B. Lamar asked for a land endowment to establish a university, and in 1839 he was given 221,240 acres for the establishment of not one, but two universities.

Meanwhile, Texas was being considered for annexation to the United States; its annexation was opposed by the North because it was feared that it would be another slave state. However, England was seeking a new source of cotton, and some in the United States feared that England might acquire Texas. Under this vacillation in Congress, Secretary of State Calhoun concluded a treaty of annexation with the Republic of Texas. Presidential candidates took their stands: Henry Clay felt that annexation would result in war with Mexico and he opposed it; Martin VanBuren also opposed annexation; President Tyler favored annexation on the grounds stated above. The U.S. Senate defeated the treaty and the issue became a hot one in the election campaign. When Tyler won the election of 1844, he was able to secure passage of the treaty with the following provisions:

1. Texas was annexed as a state, not as a territory.
2. Texas public lands were retained by the state (in exchange, Texas was to pay its own public debt rather than have this taken over by the United States).
3. Texas might later, if it chose, divide itself into as many as five states.

Under the Compromise of 1850, however, the United States agreed to pay the public debt of Texas and Texas was left debt-free *and* in control of its own public lands.

The land grant approved in 1839 was actually given in 1856 when the new state legislature called for a survey of the lands. Some 216,805 acres were actually set aside for the universities. In the midst of some controversy, the University of Texas was approved by legislative act in 1858, but secession and the Civil War prevented its actual founding. After the Civil War, the Constitution of Texas of 1866 reconfirmed the land grants that had been set aside earlier. However, in the Constitution of 1876 the state land grant was reconfirmed, and the Agricultural and Mechanical College of Texas was founded, but an earlier railroad land grant was replaced with a million acres of arid West Texas land. "Friends of the university" objected and in 1883 the legislature appropriated still more land so that the total in the Permanent University Fund became 2,100,000 acres.

At the dedication of the cornerstone of the west wing of the Main Building of the University of Texas on November 17, 1882, Ashbel Smith said, "Smite the rocks with the rod of knowledge, and fountains of unstinted wealth will gush forth." In 1923 oil was discovered on university land and the Permanent University Fund became immensely large.

Texas A & M University was originally one of the two schools in the University of Texas System and shared in the income from the Permanent University Fund (known as the Available Fund). However, Texas A & M sought appropriations from the legislature, instead of utilizing its endowment, and so dropped out of the fund. After the discovery of oil, Texas A & M sued for readmission and was awarded a one-third interest in the fund. The A & M of Texas now is a university system, with Texas A & M University at its head, paralleling the University of Texas system.

Three pioneers in America were largely responsible for the establishment of the land-grant colleges.* Jonathan Baldwin Turner of Illinois College proposed that there should be a university for the industrial classes in each state and that such colleges should have connected with them lands that could be used for experimental purposes. Thomas Green Clemson worked for the establishing of agricultural colleges in the South supported by land grants; he was the founder of Clemson Agricultural College through a bequest in his will which South Carolina accepted in 1889. Justin Smith Morrill

---

* Information in this section taken mostly from *A Century of Higher Education* by William W. Brickman and Stanley Lehrer. (Westport, Connecticut: Greenwood Press, Publishers, 1962).

first introduced a land-grant bill in the House of Representatives on December 14, 1857. The bill was passed by the House and by the Senate, but President Buchanan vetoed it on February 24, 1859 for the following reasons: the federal government was in financial straits, the bill would pose a danger to states' rights, it was potentially dangerous to new states, the advancement of agriculture and mechanic arts was a disputed issue in the country, there might be unfavorable results of the bill for existing colleges, and it was unconstitutional.

The Civil War and the attitudes of President Lincoln changed the picture and when the act was proposed again in 1861 it passed and was signed into law. Known as "An act donating public lands to the several states and territories which may provide colleges for the benefit of agriculture and the mechanic arts," the first Morrill Act provided 30,000 acres of federal land to each state for each senator and representative, as indicated earlier.

In 1887 the Hatch Act (properly called the Hatch Experiment Station Act) was passed and signed into law. Under this act the federal government was to furnish annual appropriations of $15,000 to each state for the establishment of agricultural experiment stations at the land-grant institutions. The second Morrill Act, passed in 1890, provided an initial appropriation to each state of $15,000 to increase the endowment or support of the land-grant colleges, this amount was to increase in annual increments to a maximum of $25,000. (It was this act, alluded to elsewhere in this book, that allowed the "separate but equal" institutions for Negroes.) In 1907 the Nelson Amendment to the Morrill Acts of 1862 and 1890 provided for the addition of $5,000 per year for five years to the original land-grant funding. The Smith-Lever Act, passed in 1914, authorized the land-grant institutions to offer extension work away from the campus and so set up the agricultural and home economics extension services that became very popular throughout the country and that still are popular (and useful) today. Finally, the Bankhead-Jones Act, passed in 1935, added still more funds to the annual appropriations for the support of A & M colleges to allow for agricultural research and for co-operative agricultural extension work.

Completion of this story is in the Smith-Hughes Act of 1917 which established vocational agriculture and home economics programs in secondary schools. These programs (that is, their instructors) operate cooperatively with the other land-grant programs in a sort of interlocking management and information system that also includes the 4-H clubs for young people.

Cornell University may have been the result of an awful lot of serendipity. Andrew D. White had impressions both of the American college (from Yale where he had studied) and of European universities (he visited Oxford and Cambridge and had attended the Sorbonne and the University of Berlin). He also was influenced by the ideas of Henry Tappan when he was a freshman at Michigan. He conceived the idea of an American university free from sectarian and/or party control, peopled with learned professors, offering both classical and more practical programs, and physically conducive to learning (with towers, galleries, museums, laboratories, lecture halls and the like).

In 1864 White became a New York state senator and was chosen to be chairman of the committee on education. Ezra Cornell was chairman in the same senate of the committee on agriculture. Cornell was wealthy, having invested and worked his way up to being the largest stockholder in Western Union. Meanwhile, the Morrill Act of 1862 had been passed and signed into law, and New York was considering the founding of an appropriate A & M college. In 1865 White presented a speech before the New York state senate urging them not to split the land grant (as they were considering doing) between a new People's College and an old but ineffective State Agricultural College. Instead, he urged the founding of a school: (1) concentrating all available financial support, (2) state regulated and not in any way sectarian, and (3) tied closely to the whole state system of education — through the awarding of scholarships for students from other state schools to attend the new institution.

Ezra Cornell wanted to use his wealth to benefit the "industrial, laboring, and productive" classes of people in New York. White, in effect, persuaded him to help found the new college, along with use of the available land-grant funds. Cornell's famous statement, "I would found an institution in which any person can find instruction in any study," became the guide for the new school. (White had suggested a school to prepare "captains in the army of industry.") Cornell University was chartered in 1865 and White became its organizing president; he was formally elected to that office in 1867. The school opened in 1869 with one building completed, seventeen resident professors, and eight nonresident professors. The latter was an idea of White's to get the most prominent people in various fields on his faculty without actually having to entice them to stop what they were doing and move to Ithaca. The school had 400 students (50 applicants had actually been rejected). In his innaugural address White stressed that: (1) there was no caste system at Cornell, all courses of study were equally prestigious; (2) students would provide manual labor at the college both to help in their own support and to acquire valuable educational experience; (3) scientific studies would be emphasized both as sciences and as appropriate procedures in all fields of knowledge; and (4) the real purpose of education was to develop individuals, in the fullest sense, for useful roles in society. The overall idea was to have the university embody a spirit of free and universal inquiry to serve scholarship in all areas.

The trustees served limited terms of five years (definitely not the life terms of trustees in earlier institutions) and were elected by the alumni (certainly not self-perpetuating). The university had two divisions: (1) the division of special sciences and arts, which had nine departments, including agriculture, mechanic arts, medicine, law, and education, and (2) the division of science, literature and the arts. There were five different general programs and one that was totally elective (copied after Michigan). Thus, there were five options for general education and nine vocational or professional paths a student could follow. There was no school of theology and this led to attacks on Cornell from older, more prestigious schools.

As early as 1862 Andrew White had proposed admitting women and "colored persons" to the new university. A women's dormitory was built with private funds and women were admitted beginning in 1872; however, black students were not admitted until nearly one hundred years later.

The higher education of Negroes began early in our history. In 1774 Ezra Stiles (before he became president of Yale) arranged for two black men, Bristol Yamma and John Quamine, to be educated at the (then) College of New Jersey, Princeton. The Presbyterian

Church took the lead in establishing institutions for Negroes; in 1816 a school was begun at Parsippany, New Jersey, but it was not successful. But in 1854 Ashmun Institute (later Lincoln University) was opened in Pennsylvania. Oberlin College (in Ohio) admitted Negro students as did Bowdoin and Amherst and Knox College.

Of course, the events preceding the Civil War in the South prevented higher education for Negroes in that section of the country; indeed, it was illegal for some time even to educate Negro slaves in reading and writing. However, under the leadership of the Congregational Church, a school was set up at Hampton, Virginia, on September 17, 1861 (almost immediately after the town was taken over by northern troops). This school was for children, but it grew into the Hampton Institute (1867); this college now offers bachelor's and master's degrees in liberal arts, teacher education, architecture, nursing, and engineering and has a faculty of some 200 with 3,000 students. Talladega College (near Birmingham, Alabama) was founded in 1867 also and Fisk University in Nashville in 1866. The Negro college that most people recognize immediately is Tuskegee Institute. This school was founded by Booker T. Washington in 1881 (at Tuskegee, near Montgomery, Alabama).

Also among the early black colleges were: Avery College in Allegheny City, Pennsylvania (1849), Morehouse in New York (1867), Meharry Medical College in Nashville, Tennessee (1917), and Howard University in Washington, D.C. (1917).

The second Morrill Act, passed in 1890, encouraged the establishing of separate colleges for Negroes, in that it provided that none of the appropriated funds should be awarded to a college where racial distinction was made in admissions, *except* that if there existed separate facilities for Negro and white students, this fact was to be considered compliance with the requirement of nondistinction. An example of such facilities is the Normal School for Colored Teachers founded in 1876 at the small town of Prairie View, some 50 miles northwest of Houston, Texas. The name was changed in 1889 to Prairie View State Normal and Industrial College, adding programs in agriculture and home economics and industrial areas. In 1947 the college became Prairie View A & M University, a unit of the Texas A & M University System.

Early schools for American Indians, however, tended to be either

low-level institutions (elementary or high schools at best) or specialized schools, e.g., for art training. There were the Carlisle Indian
School (1879), Haskell Institute in Lawrence, Kansas, Sherman Institute in California, Bacone College in Muscogee, Oklahoma, and
the Santa Fe Indian School.

A more recent college for the Navajo Indians opened in 1969 at
Many Farms, Arizona. Navajo Community College began in bor-
rowed quarters but soon moved to permanent buildings outside
Many Farms (about 25 miles from Gallup, New Mexico). The
Navajos, of course, are under the Bureau of Indian Affairs, but they
do have their own tribal government, the Navajo Tribal Council,
elected by the members of the tribe. It was this council that decided
to open a college for reservation youth, and the college is responsible
to the council for its results. There is a board of regents, all Navajo,
and the first president was Ned A. Hatathli, also Navajo.

Entrance requirements at NCC are like those at most community
colleges, except that one does not have to have a high school diploma
if he/she is at least 18 years old. Also, like other community colleges,
it offers an AA program for students who desire to transfer to a four-
year school, a vocational-technical program, a program in Navajo
studies (including silversmithing, an adopted Navajo art), and a
precollege program, as well as continuing education courses for
adults. Essentially, the college is a conservative institution with the
purpose of providing an education for Navajo youth under the direction of Navajos themselves.

In contrast with NCC, Pima College in Tucson, Arizona is an in-
novative school offering a veritable smorgasbord of courses and programs. It started in 1970 and is supported by Pima County and the
state of Arizona. It is open to anybody and the actual student body is
extremely varied; those who might benefit greatly from this new
school, however, are not as heavily represented as was desired. The
Pima, Papago, and Yaqui Indians of the Tucson area represent only
about 2 percent of the student body.

Still another community college that serves an Indian population
in part is Flathead Community College in Kalispell, Montana. This
college was approved by the local voters in 1967 and serves the
whole community, including Blackfoot Indians from a nearby reservation.

Cornell did not pioneer the higher education of women, although it was an early leader as noted. Wesleyan Female College had been founded in Macon, Georgia in 1836. Oberlin College (chartered in 1834 at Oberlin, Ohio) admitted women immediately. Wisconsin admitted women in 1863; Vassar was founded (for women) in 1861. Women's suffrage in America began in 1869. Further founding of women's colleges followed: Wellesley in 1875, Smith in 1875, Radcliffe (as the Society for the Collegiate Instruction of Women) in 1879, and Pembroke in 1891.

Cornell and her sister land-grant institutions also pioneered in military training. At Cornell, military training was compulsory for all general course students (those who were in what we would call a liberal arts program today) but optional for others. White also tried to encourage shared student-faculty seminars and cultural mingling. This, with the utilization of scientific procedures in research, the breadth of programs, the elective possibilities, and the "Cornell Plan" created a university with many aspects of the great European schools but yet peculiar to the New World. The so-called Cornell Plan included:

1. an all-purpose curriculum
2. equality among subjects, courses, and curricula
3. scientific research
4. service to society through the study of commerce, government, and human relations
5. openness to all classes of students as follows:
   a. graduates of secondary schools could attend the college
   b. the "most brilliant" high school graduates would receive scholarships
   c. outstanding university graduates would receive fellowships for three more years of study, either at Cornell or elsewhere
   d. the top graduate scholars would receive special stipends to continue to study the "most difficult problems facing the nation and the world"

Cornell caught the minds of Americans almost immediately. With its practical tone, yet with an emphasis on basic research as also important, with its openness to all groups, including women, and with its non-sectarian governance, it appealed to all. When Ezra Cornell was criticized for his handling of the endowments, there resulted an outpouring of additional gifts. Professorships of Hebrew, of oriental literature, and of history were established by donors. In 1889 a journalist said of Cornell, "With a grip on the best methods of education which is almost beyond the reach of an institution weighed down by traditions...Cornell University stands in the vantage ground, if not at the head, of American educational institutions." Cornell provided a model for other institutions: Minnesota under its president, Will W. Folwell, in 1869 copied Cornell almost entirely; Wisconsin followed her lead but developed the service aspect to a special peak. Cornell also provided the spur for still another new experiment, the graduate schools, Johns Hopkins, Clark, Catholic University in Washington, D.C., Bryn Mawr, and ultimately Chicago.

Most if not all of the A & M's had military units or were run entirely in a military fashion. For example, Cornell at first required its students to wear uniforms and to march to and from campus functions. This tradition did not continue long, becoming modified after student complaints grew loud, but nevertheless the other A & M's followed the lead of Cornell and instituted some sort of military training. (Texas A & M University still has its proud "Corps of Cadets" as do many other institutions.)

However, military training for officers in the United States service had begun quite a bit earlier. The U.S. Military Academy at West Point (New York) had been opened in 1802. Cadets were admitted to the academy upon recommendation (nomination, actually, since they also had to qualify academically) by a member of Congress. Currently, the academy admits perhaps 1,000 cadets annually upon congressional recommendations (each senator and representative is allowed to have five cadets at the academy at any given time) and some 400 to 500 through competitive applications from army personnel, children of deceased or disabled army veterans, and honor graduates of military schools. Cadets are provided room and board and all regular living expenses (tuition is not charged) and, in addition, they earn annual salaries. In return, graduates must spend at least five years in the regular army immediately following graduation.

The second of the military service institutions was the U.S. Naval Academy at Annapolis (Maryland), founded in 1845, and the third was the U.S. Coast Guard Academy at New London (Connecticut), founded in 1876. The latter institution opened after the Civil War, of course, and it had been preceded by a southern military academy. What is now The Citadel had been founded in Charlotte, South Carolina, in 1842, also predating the Naval Academy by three years. Midshipmen are admitted to the Naval Academy upon nomination by congressmen or other governmental persons authorized to make nominations. As with the military academy, midshipmen are also admitted from among the children of deceased or disabled veterans, honor military school graduates, and from ROTC units. However, a limited number of midshipmen also come from Puerto Rico, the Phillipines, and from Canada, depending upon the openings available each year. Women are admitted in limited numbers to both academies. The Naval Academy serves both the navy and the marines. As with the military academy, the naval academy provides living quarters and certain other necessities as well as a monthly salary to midshipmen.

The U.S. Coast Guard Academy admits students competitively (competition includes extracurricular activities in high school as well as grades and test performance); there are no congressional nominations. In addition to having to pay no tuition or other living expenses, cadets are allowed $4,000 annually against which they can draw for uniforms, textbooks, etc. Graduates receive commissions as ensigns in the Coast Guard and bachelor's degrees.

In 1938 the federal government also established the U.S. Merchant Marine Academy at Kings Point (New York). Admission is only through congressional nominations based on state quotas according to population. While there is no salary at this academy, cadets are provided all necessities, including uniforms and textbooks as well as living quarters, medical and dental services, food, etc. However, half of the junior and senior years are spent in actual shipboard service, and the cadets do receive pay for this time. Unlike the other academies described, the U.S. Merchant Marine Academy does not automatically grant commissions to its graduates. They receive the bachelor's degree, but they must apply for commissions in the U.S. Naval Reserve and pass whatever examinations are required for licenses as mates or engineers on merchant ships. A limited number of cadets are admitted from Latin America, as well as from the Phillipines and other U.S. territories.

The latest of the military academies to open was the U.S. Air Force Academy at Colorado Springs (Colorado), founded in 1954. This academy followed the example of West Point, in that cadets are admitted upon congressional recommendation, with each senator and representative allowed up to five cadets in the academy at any given time. Additional cadets are admitted through competition. Women are eligible; in this academy non-United States citizens are not admitted, however. Graduates are commissioned as second lieutenants in the Air Force and they may enter pilot training after graduation (this is not included in the academy's program).

South Carolina's military school (now The Citadel) opened as a military school attached to the Arsenal Academy to prepare officers for the military service. The year 1842 marked a period of unrest in the nation and which reached enough of a peak that southern states were considering at least the possibility of secession and so it seemed appropriate to begin preparations for a trained military. The school was closed in 1865 but reopened in 1882 as South Carolina Military Academy; it became The Citadel in 1910. It remains a men's school and is run on a military basis — barracks living, military discipline, uniforms, etc. Graduates, however, receive a B.A. or B.S. degree and not a military commission.

Following the Civil War the great state universities began their growth. In part, of course, this was due to the passage of the Morrill Act and succeeding legislation and in part it was due to recognition by states that their universities could truly be of service. This recognition seems to have come earliest and most pronouncedly in the Midwest — Illinois, Michigan, Minnesota, and Wisconsin. At the close of the Civil War the University of Wisconsin was a relatively small school; it had been founded in 1848 as a non-denominational seminary. When Morrill Act funds were allocated to this institution, it began a period of immediate and dramatic change.

American history students associate Wisconsin (back when it was only the Wisconsin Territory) with the Dred Scott case. Doctor John Emerson of St. Louis traveled the country as an army surgeon and spent periods of time in Illinois, Wisconsin, and Missouri. His slave, Dred Scott, accompanied him and when Emerson died in 1846 Scott sued for his liberty on the grounds that slavery had been forbidden in Wisconsin when he resided there. In 1857 (James Buchanan was president of the country) the United States Supreme Court ruled that Scott was not free, that he could not even sue in federal court since he was not a citizen, and that the Missouri Compromise, which had forbidden slavery in the Wisconsin Territory, was unconstitutional since it would have deprived a person (Emerson) of his property (Scott) without due process of law.

This historical note, of course, had little to do with the state of Wisconsin which was admitted to the Union in 1848 and immediately founded its land-grant university. During the pre-Civil War railroad expansion, Wisconsin had been "opened" to traffic but much of the state remained rural. Settlement was by New Englanders (who brought with them an educational zeal), by German immigrants (who brought respect for the learning tradition of the German universities), and by Scandinavians (who were cooperative and politically aggressive). Thus, in contrast with the prevailing frontier attitude toward education, the Wisconsin public held the process and the professors involved in higher education in high regard.

The post-Civil War "progressive movement" (a bit like today's "moral majority" movement) sought to purify life by establishing middle-class morality, by protecting the weak, and by controlling big business. This movement reached a peak in Wisconsin under Governor Robert LaFollette around 1900-1912. LaFollette was a graduate of the University of Wisconsin and he was determined that the university should work closely with the state government and vice versa. He was able to get Charles R. VanHise, also of Wisconsin, appointed president of the university in 1904. In addition to being a progressive, VanHise had been influenced by the Chautauqua movement ideas pushed by Wm. Rainey Harper when he was a visiting lecturer at Chicago.

Meanwhile, wheat farming in Wisconsin had given way to dairying. Under VanHise, the University of Wisconsin started a program of short courses on agricultural topics, courses offered in the field, and these rapidly increased agricultural productivity in the state. Research at the university also centered on agricultural production; development of the "Babcock fat test" resulted in savings (hence profits) of hundreds of millions of dollars to the state's diary industry. The people of Wisconsin came to identify the university as *their* school. Extension programs expanded; by 1910 over 5,000 people were enrolled in correspondence courses, and district extension centers were opened all over the state. A Bureau of General Welfare was opened as a sort of information center to answer questions from citizens about practically anything (emphasis on agricultural topics). A Bureau of Debating and Public Discussion sponsored local discussion groups and provided a kind of travelling lending library for books. The state became the campus of the university.

LaFollette was a political "boss," a showman, a bit paranoid, but he also trusted knowledge and he surrounded himself with experts as they were needed. A sort of interlocking directorate developed between the state university and the state government. By 1910, 35 professors were assigned part time to various state commissions; political scientists helped draft legislation, university engineers helped to plan roads and buildings, agricultural scientists continued to advance the dairying industry, and VanHise himself served on five or six commissions at any given time. The Saturday Lunch Club in Madison brought together professors and legislators for a weekly exchange of views. The total program came to be known as the Wisconsin Idea and served as a model for many other states to follow, especially with regard to the services provided by the university to citizens for very practical purposes.

Thus, the state universities were products of at least three movements. The first was the post-Civil War effort to find institutional expression for the Age of Reason and for the developing nationalism in the country. The second movement was the westward expansion of the population, and the third was the agricultural and mechanical expansion following passage of the Morrill Acts and related legislation. It actually remained for the American high school to finally make the state universities the democratic institutions that they have become. (Certification of high schools developed generally throughout the Midwest so that by 1890 the high schools were the practical route to the university.)

Following the Civil War American colleges underwent a period of great changes. The Morrill Act and its later related acts were responsible for much of this change, but in addition there was a whole new spirit in the land. More parents could afford to send their boys (primarily) to college and more youth wanted to go to college. Programs had moved toward more practical expectations and purposes and this became even more pronounced following the development of land-grant institutions. Many wealthy men, a lot of them with railroad wealth, were willing to invest in colleges. And teaching procedures were advancing from the old patterns to newer ones that were more suited for the education of larger numbers of students.

Harvard was at the forefront of the movement. Charles William Eliot assumed the presidency in 1869 and began expanding the course offerings. He increased the available courses in modern languages, economics, and the sciences. He raised the standards of the medical school, he introduced the case study method in the law school, and he encouraged his faculty to experiment with teaching procedures. He allowed students to take books out of the library rather than having to use them under direct supervision. And, as we will see later, he introduced the elective system. Harvard moved toward becoming a university but only in its basic undergraduate offerings.

Johns Hopkins and Chicago both specialized in actual graduate education and these were the real movers toward universities in America. (Chicago was modeled after Hopkins.) Cornell, first among the land-grant institutions, set the pattern for still further development. The land-grant universities were quick to pick up on new ideas. Most were coeducational and offered a wide variety of courses, in addition to the basic agriculture and mechanic arts. They also got into the business of extension courses and summer programs (begun by William Rainey Harper at Chicago).

Not all was good in the growth of institutions in the late 1800s. The elective system went too far and had to be pulled back to something like it is now — partial electives following specified basic programs. Boards of regents were more and more populated with businessmen and in many instances these individuals exerted influences that undermined the academic activities of a school. Alumni, too, increased greatly in number and it was probably due to their influence that fraternities developed and that sports became a large part of college life. Also, as the institutions became ever larger the importance of administrators increased with an accompanying decrease in the power and prestige of professors.

Some historians say that the universities of the later 1800s were coarse and materialistic (if not hedonistic) because that was the nature of the American culture. Business and industry were the dominant influences of the time. However, there were also great cultural advances in other areas, in part due to the influence of the universities. J.W. Gibbs, a professor at Yale, invented a whole new science, physical chemistry. H.A. Rowland advanced the science of spectrum analysis and contributed much to our ideas of atomic and molecular structure. A.A. Michelson (Chicago — Rowland was at Hopkins) measured the speed of light. Richard T. Ely was a leader in developments in economics along with H.C. Adams. Herbert Spencer, an Englishman, exerted great influence on thinking in American sociology through his follower, William Graham Sumner (Yale).

John C. Calhoun and Woodrow Wilson are examples of presidents who were thinkers in this age. Calhoun was concerned with ideas such as the rights of individual states rather than with the wishes of unions or organized bodies of lobbyists or political parties. Wilson saw a distinction between essential governmental functions and those functions that could serve to better the quality of life. (His major project, the League of Nations, of course, was not destined for success.) Oliver Wendell Holmes argued for the logical application of law rather than the mechanical use of precedents. While much of the writing of the age was poor and gaudy, there were also such writing giants as Mark Twain, William Dean Howells, Stephen Crane, and Hamlin Garland.

In art, Thomas Eakins and Winslow Homer were painting realistic scenes. James A. McNeill Whistler did his "Arrangement in Grey and Black." And Mary Cassatt was among the "French impressionists," though she was American. William James essentially introduced modern psychology in his major book, *Principles of Psychology* (1890). Pragmatism was on the road and it was picked up by John Dewey, who applied the ideas to education in the beginning of the following century.

(At the risk of offending some institution) the major colleges and universities founded soon after the Civil War included:

Vassar (1865)
MIT (1865)
Howard University (1867)
University of California (1868)
University of Cincinnati (1870) (Changed from Cincinnati College, founded in 1819)
Vanderbilt (1875)
Johns Hopkins (1876)
Ohio State University (1878)
Stetson University (in Deland, Florida, 1883)
Tulane (1884)
University of Illinois (1885) (Founded as Illinois Industrial University)
Yale College became Yale University in 1887
Clark (1889)
Stanford (1891)
Chicago (1891)
College of New Jersey became Princeton University in 1896
Kings College, later Columbia College, became Columbia University in 1912

Urbanization has been a persistent movement in America. If one can identify the colonial colleges with the needs of religious sects, the frontier colleges with a variety of very specific needs, the Yankee colleges with efforts to achieve intellectual prestige, the state universities (at the beginning) with civil needs, and the A & M's with the social and industrial requirements of a developing country, there remained a void in relation to the unique needs of the cities. The first city university opened in 1837 in Charleston, South Carolina. Louisville, Kentucky, began its city university in the same year, and what became the City College of New York started as the Free Academy of New York City in 1847. Following the Civil War, the growth of cities became even more pronounced, and Cincinnati opened its university in 1873, Toledo in 1884, Akron in 1913, Detroit in 1923,

Wichita in 1926, and Omaha in 1931. (Wayne University in Detroit, Hunter College, Brooklyn College, and Queen's College in New York City were also city institutions.)

In some cases the city's needs were served by there being another institution located there — the University of Minnesota in Minneapolis, the University of California at Berkeley and at Los Angeles, Boston University, Temple University in Philadelphia, the University of Buffalo, the University of Rochester, the University of Denver, Washington University in St. Louis, George Washington University and American University in Washington, D.C., and Western Reserve in Cleveland (also Harvard, Columbia, Johns Hopkins, Stanford, the University of Pennsylvania, and the University of Chicago). Generally, the city colleges were fairly slow in developing, financially hindered, and in some cases quite expensive to operate. Essentially, they have remained fairly specific city service institutions but, nevertheless, an important part of higher education in America.

VIGNETTE

CHARLES WILLIAM ELIOT (1834-1926)

Eliot spent 40 years as president of Harvard, and under him the elective system came to full bloom. His father, Sam Eliot, had been treasurer of Harvard, and Charles enrolled there at age 15, having attended the Boston Latin School from age 10. He studied mathematics, chemistry, and mineralogy, but in his junior year his eyes failed him and he had to stop studying for several months. He finished the degree, however, and became a tutor. In 1861 he became head of the Lawrence Scientific School at Harvard, but he was denied a position that he wanted, the Rutherford Professorship, and he left for travel in England. He returned in 1865 to become professor of chemistry at Massachusetts Institute of Technology and in 1869 he was offered the presidency of Harvard.

In his inaugural address he argued for impartial admissions, for electives in the curriculum, and for degrees for women (by extension). He felt that the role of the university was to broaden and deepen the learning of its students. He opened the course structure so that restrictions to departments were removed, although he set up the administration-by-department system. He established the position of dean. He made the divinity school more "scientific," reorganized the medical and law schools, and perfected to its peak the elective system. Harvard grew greatly under his leadership, and its reputation also grew as the ability of its professors became widely known.

Eliot retired from Harvard in 1908 and spent several years as the Carnegie Emissary for Peace, traveling around the world. He died in 1926.

During the same period of our history that saw the development of the great A & M universities, another of our prominent collegiate institutions also began. The first intercollegiate football game was played in 1869 between Princeton University and Rutgers University. From this first game (which was one of the soccer type with kicking the prominent activity) football grew rapidly (with the style changing also to carrying the ball rather than kicking it). In 1889 the University of the South sent out its team for six consecutive days of competition.*

In the early history of the sport there were no regulations regarding eligibility. Faculty members could play on the team as could professional players. However, after 1890 the number of non-students on a team was limited to two per game. The Thanksgiving Day game between Yale and Princeton became a tradition around 1893. In 1905 the brutality and professional nature of football resulted in the deaths of 18 persons; Harvard had only two games without at least one concussion. The president of the United States, Theodore Roosevelt, said that if the colleges did not clean up the game he would abolish it. On October 9, 1905, coaches and physical education directors of many colleges met with President Roosevelt and agreed to undertake a movement toward control of the sport.

With control, the alumni got into the act. Alumni were willing to

---

*Rudolph, Frederick, *The American College and University, A History.* (New York: Vintage Books [Random House], 1962).

provide financial support for the game in exchange for a say in its management. This movement practically pushed faculty out of the picture as far as regulating the sport was concerned; it became essentially a separate entity within the universities. The press too played a large part in this movement by reporting the games and encouraging spectators. Football eventually became a public relations device. Tournaments developed (the first Tournament of Roses game was played, however, in 1902 between Stanford and Michigan — Michigan won 49-0). Amos Alonzo Stagg was a very important faculty member at Chicago (Stagg Field, of course, is named after him).

By the way, women were not allowed to *watch* football games until the Yale-Princeton game of 1885.

CHAPTER 4

THE DEVELOPMENT OF GRADUATE SCHOOLS

THE colleges that existed in America before and immediately after 1800 probably served the needs of the country exceptionally well, but they were almost entirely undergraduate institutions — whatever their names. A few bachelors did remain from time to time, living on campus and referred to as "resident graduates." But graduate classes were formed only if a sufficient number of such students demanded them. As early as 1643 a scholarship fund had been set up at Harvard for the M.A. but it was simply absorbed into the endowment. Colleges lacked the money to support scholarships, and the nature of the country's growth, with thin populations both in settled areas and on the frontier, resulted in the dispersal rather than the concentration in one place of men of high ability. When the University of Virginia was founded, Charles Mercer, who wrote the legislation that founded the institution, envisioned a four-level educational system: elementary school for everyone, academies for those who were to be prepared to enter college, colleges for professional preparation and for liberal arts education, and the university for the advanced study of a profession or for "the culture and pursuit of science." But Thomas Jefferson was realist enough to recognize that the University of Virginia would not accomplish all of this, because at the time there was no demand for the higher degrees.

American democracy apparently caused the founding of numerous colleges which remained relatively small in size as opposed to a few larger institutions. Had there been such larger institutions, the movement toward a true university might have occurred earlier than it did. As it was, there were those intellectuals in the colleges (most of whom had been influenced by study in Europe) who argued the need for a university — indeed, for universities — in America, saying that the colleges were just not doing what was required in this growing nation. Francis Wayland of Brown said in 1850 that the collegiate system did not serve the needs for scientific and practical study and that it did not offer opportunity for advanced study. Henry Phillip Tappan lamented that America did not aspire to advanced education; he tried to educate Michigan voters on the need for the opportunity for students to advance beyond the bachelor's degree and his arguments had a profound influence on Andrew D. White, who later was to oversee the opening of Cornell University.

Tappan placed a heavy emphasis on libraries as a component of any institution that would claim university status, saying that the constituents of a university were scholars and books. He also felt that scholars must be free to study, do research, and learn if their institution were to be called a university. While novice learners (those in colleges) needed to acquire mental discipline, mature scholars should be responsible for their own continued development. To aid in this process, the institution must maintain (in addition to a great library) a cadre of eminent scholars as professors. Tappan insisted that a government could not make a university by law, it could only charter the institution. Those charged with managing the institution also could contribute to its being a university only through their wise decisions when choosing professors.

Tappan further insisted that a university must be large, for, he said, "the very idea of a University is that of concentrating books and apparatus, and learned men in one place." He felt that the areas of human knowledge were and must be interdependent and to isolate any of them would cause it to wither. Professors and scholars must have opportunities to intercommunicate within their fields and among fields of learning. He pointed to the great European universities as examples where size did indeed seem to be associated with success and he urged the state of Michigan to forego regional jealousies and allow the university to be concentrated in one location and to grow to a size appropriate to its hoped-for greatness. Finally,

Tappan urged complete separation of the university from sectarian religious influences.

The founding of universities was delayed not only by the prevailing public attitude but also by the active opposition of church groups (of course, most of the pre-Civil War colleges were church sponsored and any new institution would constitute a threat against them). In founding Cornell, White's ideas were opposed by sectarian influences and Cornell himself was constrained to write a response to the charge that he was founding an aristocratic institution. White, in the New York legislature, also had to fight battles against those who wanted to fragment the newly available land-grant funds by awarding them to several of the smaller existing colleges in the state.

Unrest at Harvard, precipitated by some suggestions made by George Ticknor, including professorial opposition to any changes, and culminating in a student rebellion with mass dismissals, led the overseers to make some drastic alterations in Harvard's structure in 1825. In general, the school became departmentalized, provisions were made for easier curricular changes, and it was required that students be consulted regarding degree requirements. These changes may have provided seed for graduate education, but there was no immediate development of an earned master's degree program. In 1831 Charles Beck introduced the seminar as a teaching procedure at Harvard.

The university era has been identified as 1869-1902, although Cornell was founded in 1865 and Johns Hopkins not until 1876. (The period named was selected by Daniel Coit Gilman when he reviewed the accomplishments of that era in 1906.)* Gilman suggested that the beginning might have been in the founding of the Lawrence and Sheffield Scientific Schools, since this indicated a willingness on the part of two major colleges to undertake the new and advanced scientific studies. He also gave credit to the passage of the Morrill Act and the immediate founding of Cornell, and he pointed to Johns Hopkins, Chicago, Stanford, and Tulane (New Orleans, Louisiana, 1834) as institutions in which it was all right to introduce new subjects and new methods of teaching and learning. Finally, he also

---

*From Daniel Coit Gilman Reviews the Accomplishments of the University Era. 1869-1902. In Richard Hofstadter and Wilson Smith (Eds.): *American Higher Education: A Documentary History,* (Chicago: University of Chicago Press, 1961. vol. I).

gave credit for advancement to the state universities of the Northeast and the West coast.

What Gilman saw as the advancements included support for the sciences and growth of knowledge in the sciences (and the concomitant decline of the "old-fashioned" curricula), advances in historical and political sciences, requirements of modern languages instead of the ancient languages, and more emphasis on English literature. He also remarked upon changes in schools of medicine where, he said, the lecture method had declined. Gilman also said that using the name "university" hardly made an institution what its name implied. There were numerous institutions in the country that so called themselves. There were also those that were given the name gratuitously because they were for the education of black students who had never before had this opportunity (he identified Fisk, Atlanta, and Howard). Gilman suggested that a true university must have at least schools of liberal arts or philosophy, law, medicine, and theology. He also said that a university must provide the opportunity for *advanced* — as opposed to professional — study under the guidance of professors who were themselves scholars in their fields.

Efforts were exerted in New York City, at Albany, in Pennsylvania, and at Yale to move toward universities (with graduate programs), also. Plans were proposed at Columbia in 1857 for graduate education, when a committee reported, "With professors of respectable mediocrity or a little above it, a College will languish, but may subsist indefinitely. But a University cannot be planted and long maintained in life without professors of splendid name and ability, especially in a community where such institutions are unknown and where general mediocrity of attainment and aspiration is the obstacle to be removed and the evil to be remedied." Columbia's trustees passed a statute establishing an earned M.A. for two years of study beyond the B.A., but no funds were provided to "hire students." (This is a bit like the establishment of sabbaticals for university professors in the state of Texas where the legislature did pass an act establishing the sabbaticals but where subsequent legislatures have never provided funds for them.)

Henry Tappan tried to make the University of Michigan into a university and he even got a graduate program into the university catalog, but there were no takers. Tappan, of course, left Michigan and the graduate program was dropped. Frederick A.P. Barnard suggested a post-graduate course at the University of Mississippi in 1858, but this too did not come to fruition.

A part of the movement toward the university and at the same time a part of the objections to the move was the developing field of science. The sciences were not immediately introduced into existing colleges following Darwin's publication of *The Origin of Species*, although new institutions usually did include the sciences in their curricula. As has been pointed out earlier, scientific research was a key to the discovery of new knowledge and this, of course, was necessary to the development of the university in America. The setting that produced movement toward scientific research, however, was apparently anti-religious (recall earlier comments that indicated that this was not necessarily the case, although citizens of the time thought that it was the case) and this slowed the development of the university.

Meanwhile, America was growing, and she was growing rapidly. Following the Civil War the railroads in the country expanded very quickly; the track mileage record is as shown:

1865 —	35,000 miles	1880 —	93,000 miles
1870 —	52,000 miles	1890 —	167,000 miles
1875 —	74,000 miles		

Great increases in iron and steel production occurred:

1870 —	1.9 million tons	1880 —	4.3 million tons
1890 —	10.2 million tons	1900 —	15.4 million tons

Public school enrollments grew:

1870 —	6.8 million students	1880 —	10 million
1890 —	15.5 million	1900 —	compulsory attendance

Along with the growth in industry and in just plain size in America, the cultural mores underwent changes also. There developed:

1. a mild kind of consumerism, with "being cultured" a legitimate personal goal,

2. emphasis on utility in education but recognition that utilitarian outcomes often result from abstruse knowledge,
3. among the "more intellectual" a belief in liberation of the mind and in the goodness of knowledge for its own sake
4. a belief that "science can achieve anything,"
5. among the "most intellectual" a belief that the love of knowledge must not be tainted by sordid motives; enthusiasm for truth leads to an almost fanatic search for the verities,
6. in colleges and universities an increased emphasis on research and thinking (with a decreased emphasis on teaching, particularly on the mere imparting of information),
7. development of the seminar as a major mode of college instruction.

American scholars, however, were frustrated, in that there was little opportunity in this country for truly advanced study. In increasing numbers they turned to German universities for their education. For example, between 1815 and 1914 American students attended German universities to the extent of over 10,000 individuals — half of them at Berlin, the others at Leipzig, Heidelberg, Halle, Bonn, Munich, and Gottingen.

Ezra Stiles had made plans to change Yale into a university as early as 1777, but there was no money to support the idea. Yale did offer opportunity for post-M.A. study in 1847 but without a degree. In 1861 Yale awarded the first Ph.D. in the country and in 1872 it founded the graduate department of philosophy and art, thus formalizing Ph.D. training in a specific graduate school. In the same year, Harvard, under Charles Eliot, finally got going what was to become the Graduate School of Arts and Sciences. (Eliot said that the effort had started "probably in 1870 and 1871.") Columbia established a graduate faculty in 1880 and in 1907 appointed a dean over the new (officially) graduate faculties. In 1912 Columbia College became Columbia University of the City of New York.

Princeton began to move toward graduate studies in 1877, established a graduate school in 1900, and physically built a residential graduate college in 1910. It became Princeton University in 1896, 150 years after its founding as the College of New Jersey. Meanwhile, of course, Cornell, Minnesota, Purdue, and Wisconsin were developing as universities but still without a major emphasis on post-M.A. level studies.

Daniel Coit Gilman had helped to plan the Sheffield Scientific School at Yale. He became president of the University of California in 1872. When the trustees of Johns Hopkins sought a president for this new university, Gilman was independently recommended by Andrew White of Cornell, Charles Eliot of Harvard, Noah Porter of Yale, and James Angell of Michigan. Johns Hopkins University was incorporated in 1867, but Hopkins' will (which provided the money for the new school) wasn't probated until 1874. Immediately in that year trustees were appointed and they began planning the school — it opened in 1876. The trustees decided that the time was ripe for a German-style graduate university in America. (President Angell had told them that they should do something new and different from what already existed in America. Hopkins' fortune, by the way, had come from investments in the Baltimore and Ohio Railroad.)

The plan at Hopkins was to have an undergraduate program but to concentrate on the graduate school, at least in terms of hiring scholars as professors. Scientific research and productive scholarship were to be the hallmark of the university. Gilman set out to hire the foremost scholars in the world and bring them to Baltimore. He got Ira Remsen (a chemist) from Williams College; Remsen had been refused a laboratory at Williams with the statement, "You will please keep in mind that this is a college and not a technical school." And he got Francis J. Child, a Chaucerian scholar, from Harvard, an eminent Greek scholar from the University of Virginia, a physicist from Rensselaer Polytechnic Institute, and a mathematician and a biologist (a student of Thomas Huxley) from England. Gilman had said that he preferred to spend the Hopkins' money for "men, not bricks and mortar," and the university developed as a faculty-centered institution. The work of the faculty was what was considered important and the faculty were given only those students who were well prepared and who could provide stimulation for research. There was not a campus, although there were plenty of facilities for research in what looked more like a factory or large store than a university. (There also were no athletic fields.) The first students were literally hired, with scholarship funds, and they included Frederick J. Turner, John Dewey, James McKeen Cattell, and Woodrow Wilson. In 1876 there were 54 graduate students and 35 undergraduates; in 1880, 102 and 37; in 1885, 184 and 96; and in 1895, 406 and 149. A study in 1926 showed that of 1,000 distinguished American scientists, 243 were Hopkins graduates. By 1896 over 60 American colleges and universities had three or more faculty members who had graduated from Hopkins; Harvard had ten, Columbia thirteen, and Wisconsin nineteen.

VIGNETTE

Daniel Coit Gilman (1831-1908)

Gilman is known as the great American educational executive, a model for successors. He attended Norwich (Connecticut) Academy and Yale, graduating in 1852 and finishing an M.A. in one more year. He became friends with Andrew White, and the two traveled to Europe to work and to study the educational systems in Russia, France, and England. He accepted a position at Yale in 1855 to assist in developing the Sheffield Scientific School; he became its assistant librarian, adding some 70,000 volumes to the collection and starting two academic societies. While at Yale, Gilman became a member of the New Haven School Board, created a high school, and reorganized the normal school. He was appointed to the board of the Sheffield School in 1866, but he left Yale in 1872 to become president of the University of California. He spent two years trying to move that university out of the politics in which it had become embroiled, and in 1874 he learned of the impending opening of Johns Hopkins University. Upon the recommendation of several prominent educators of the day (including Andrew White, his friend, and James B. Angell), Gilman was invited to serve as the first president of Hopkins; he accepted and began this work in 1874.

It was Gilman's idea to make Johns Hopkins a true graduate institution with top-level professors, quality research programs, and only minimal undergraduate offerings. He insisted upon an inquisitive spirit in his professors and that they publish the results of their research. To assist in this movement, he founded the university press and several journals. At the same time, he modified current plans for the bachelor's degree so that Baltimore youth could obtain this degree in only two years at Johns Hopkins.

Unfortunately, for the university, the Baltimore and Ohio Railroad suspended dividends in 1899 and this cut into the funds of the school very drastically. The institution began a decline until 1890 when its medical school was opened. Gilman retired in 1901 to work with the Carnegie Fund. He wrote books, served as trustee for foundations, worked on a committee to settle the boundary dispute between Venezuela and Guiana, and started the Russel Sage Foundation. He died in 1908.

Johns Hopkins was the model of a research university, eventually copied by all "great" universities in the land. And the Hopkins research ideal, coupled with the Cornell service ideal and breadth of programs, eventually provided the model for the great state universities — whether land-grant institutions or not. (The major-minor curriculum plan, by the way, came from Hopkins — the general studies idea from Cornell.) Under the leadership of Hopkins in the preparation of university professors, the doctorate became the necessary credential for university teaching, especially in the new profession of "professing" which combined teaching and research (and publication) if one was to be considered a scholar. And the offering of the doctorate, along with the accompanying research programs, became the mark that made an institution a *university*. Johns Hopkins was a great institution for only two-and-one-half decades. Its investments in the B & O Railroad lost money, Gilman retired in 1901, and Johns Hopkins became more or less just another small university.

While Johns Hopkins was the first true university in America, it certainly was not alone in developing the new graduate programs. Clark University, short lived though its graduate program was, made a contribution and so did Vanderbilt (founded in 1875), Tulane (1884), Stanford (1891), and Chicago. Among the oldest of the colonial and early American colleges to get involved in graduate education were Columbia, Princeton, Yale, and the University of

Pennsylvania. However, Harvard was the real leader in the movement, under dynamic president, Charles William Eliot. Harvard had the Lawrence Scientific School before Eliot became president, but under his leadership this school expanded and schools of arts and science, of applied science, and of business administration were added at the graduate level. The student body also increased greatly and the endowment was multipled eight times.

The chief imitator of Johns Hopkins was Clark University. Jonas Gilman Clark, a millionaire, founded Clark University in Worcester, Massachusetts in 1889 as the first *totally graduate* school in the country. G. Stanley Hall was the first president of Clark, having moved there from Hopkins. Hall was a psychologist and educator and he founded both the *American Journal of Psychology* (1887) and the American Psychological Association (1891). Under Hall, Clark University emphasized the sciences, mathematics, and psychology. It was an exceptionally open institution. According to L.M. Terman in 1903, there was no red tape. Registration consisted of giving one's name and address to an assigned thesis professor. There were no class lists, no grades; professors lectured whenever they chose. The library purchased any book requested. A student took examinations whenever his thesis professor said he was ready to do so and he graduated when he had written and successfully defended a thesis. Clark lasted only about fifteen years, however. President Hall and the university benefactor (Clark) disagreed on policies — in particular, on the addition of undergraduate programs which Hall proposed. There was also much dissension among the faculty, due in part to the vacillating funding policies of J.G. Clark. In 1892, William Rainey Harper, president of the building University of Chicago, raided Clark's faculty of all its top people (and of many not so "top").

VIGNETTE

G. STANLEY HALL (1844-1924)

Hall studied religion at Williams College (B.A.) and at Union Theological Seminary, finishing in 1868, but he was not enthusiastic about the ministry. He studied in

Germany for three years and returned to teach at Antioch College in 1871. There he read a book by Wilhelm Wundt on experimental psychology and this excited Hall to the point that he decided upon this as his field of work. When he was offered a position at Harvard in 1876, he went there to work with William James and he received the first American Ph.D. from that college in 1878 (in psychology). In 1883 he was offered the chair of psychology at Johns Hopkins and there he opened a psychology laboratory, where John Dewey was one of his students. He published widely — 14 books and some 400 other items — on childhood, adolescence, child-centered schools, and child development. Some of his publications were controversial for the time; Hall was known as an inspiring teacher, causing his students to think about what they were being taught. At Johns Hopkins, Hall founded the *American Journal of Psychology* in 1887 and what was to become the *Journal of Genetic Psychology*. He was selected as the first president, and so helped in the founding, of Clark University.

Apparently, William Rainey Harper had some difficulty in enticing learned men to Chicago because they feared becoming involved in this "Standard Oil college."* In the face of this problem Harper learned that many of the faculty at Clark University had become dissatisfied (primarily because of the vacillations of the benefactor, Clark) and might be willing to consider leaving that institution. Taking quick advantage of this opportunity, Harper made a trip to Worcester without even informing Hall of his coming. He met with a large group of the faculty and made them offers of salaries approaching double what they were paid at Clark; many accepted. Harper then went to Hall and made him the same offer; Hall refused.

Hall, of course, was furious. He argued that Harper at least owed him the duty of leaving some of the best scholars at Clark (and, incidentally, of taking some who were not so great instead). Hall even threatened to appeal to the public and directly to Rockefeller if Harper would not agree to this move. Harper agreed and did leave

---

*G. Stanley Hall Describes William R. Harper's Raid upon the Clark Faculty, 1892. *American Higher Education: A Documentary History*. Edited by R. Hofstadler and W. Smith. The University of Chicago Press, 1961.

behind some men whom he had initially wanted and took a few whom he really did not want. However, he informed all that the changes were due to bargaining with Hall. In Hall's words, "Clark had served as a nursery, for most of our faculty were simply transplanted to a richer financial soil."

Actually, another graduate school, Bryn Mawr (in Philadelphia) had been chartered in 1885 and became a college in 1888, pre-dating Clark. Bryn Mawr was intended to be a Johns Hopkins for women, but it was ahead of its time. Also a Catholic school in Washington, D.C., the Catholic University of America (1889), tried the Hopkins' model, but it plays only a minor role in the history of the time since its only graduate school was in theology. (And, incidentally, Vanderbilt in 1893 led Tulane, Duke, and Emory in becoming southern universities in the Hopkins-Cornell style.)

The university that followed the lead of Hopkins and that went on to be a continuing major institution for graduate study was the University of Chicago (1892). The "cast of characters" in its founding included John D. Rockefeller (with Standard Oil wealth), a Baptist ready to "do good works" with his money, Thomas W. Goodspeed, secretary of the Baptist Union Theological Seminary in Chicago (he encouraged the wealthy in Chicago to support the new university), Augustus H. Strong of the Rochester Theological Seminary (who encouraged Rockefeller to invest in the Chicago institution), Frederick T. Gates, secretary of the American Baptist Education Society (who "held off" the many small and hungry Baptist colleges and became the fund raiser for the new university), and William Rainey Harper, a 32-year-old Baptist layman and Hebrew scholar, and Yale professor. Rockefeller at first gave $600,000 to found the university, which was to be non-sectarian (trustees were deliberately careful to avoid any possible sectarian influence). Harper was hired to plan the school and, as indicated, Gates became its fund raiser. Eventually, through a sort of Chicago-Rockefeller rivalry encouraged by Gates and Harper, Rockefeller gave $35 million and Chicago donors provided $8 million worth of land and buildings. The university opened with a faculty of 120, and 742 students from 33 states and 15 foreign countries and provinces (328 undergraduates, 210 graduates, 204 divinity students).

VIGNETTE

WILLIAM RAINEY HARPER (1856-1906)

Born in New Concord, Ohio of Scotch-Irish parents, Harper entered college at age ten and graduated with honors at age fourteen. At age seventeen he entered Yale as a graduate student and received his Ph.D. before his nineteenth birthday in 1875. At age twenty-two he filled the chair of Hebrew studies at Morgan Park Theological Seminary; his field of research was Hebrew culture and history and he continued this research even after he became president of the University of Chicago. At one point in his early career he opened a summer school, and later he took this idea with him to Chicago. He took a position in the Yale graduate and divinity schools, teaching Hebrew, in 1881 and in 1891 he became president (first president) of the University of Chicago. He was the moving force in the initial arrangements at Chicago, in the building, in the organization, in the academic plans, and in the hiring of faculty. (His "selling" of Chicago as a potentially great institution was so effective that there were nine men in the first faculty group who had been presidents of other institutions, including James B. Angell from Michigan.)

In Harper's view a professor must be able to teach, do research, publish, and motivate students. His heavy emphasis on scholarship served to move the new university forward, both in terms of its reputation and in terms of its student enrollments. In 1886-87, the fourth year of its operation, Chicago had over 1,000 students — more than Harvard. Harper also believed that students should have a role in the governance of a university, and he tried to get them involved. He also encouraged athletics, both as an academic area and in the form of competitive teams (under Coach Amos Alonzo Stagg).

At Chicago, Harper introduced summer school, university extension, and provision for speedier graduation. He also arranged for working people to take courses at the university on a part-time basis. As seen in the text, he also encouraged the first junior college, which was inspired by the two-and-two arrangement of the undergraduate years at Chicago.

There were five main divisions at Chicago: (1) the University Proper, (2) the University Extension, (3) the University Press, (4) the University Libraries, Laboratories, and Museums, and (5) the Affiliations. The year was divided into four quarters and students could take a minimum of three quarters per year or an accelerated four quarters. The undergraduate years were divided in half — two years of junior college or "academic college" and two years of senior college or "university college."

The system of majors and minors was adopted from Johns Hopkins. At the graduate level, especially, but also in the university college, "the work of investigation was primary, the work of giving instruction secondary." Harper himself did research and taught classes. Promotion of faculty members depended on research and publication. Under Harper, ten scholarly journals were begun at Chicago, including the *Journal of Political Economy,* the *Journal of Geology,* the *School Review,* and the *American Journal of Sociology.* The faculty managed all academic affairs and could institute new programs or change courses by simple majority vote. The trustees managed the finances and maintained a "hands-off" policy with regard to academic matters.

There was a complex rank system, from head professor, to professor, non-resident professor, associate professor, assistant professor, instructor, tutor, docent, reader, lecturer, fellow, scholar. Administratively, the hierarchy was president, examiner, recorder, registrar, secretary, librarian, publisher, steward, dean, department head. (President James Angell had left the University of Wisconsin to become head of the Department of Geology at Chicago, a relatively low position in the administrative line.)

University extension eventually developed correspondence courses as well as field courses. The degree, associate of arts, was attached to the completion of the two years of junior college. The modes of instruction centered on the seminar, the laboratory, and the scholarly lecture.

It appears as though, by the late 1800s, a professor was required to have some graduate study to obtain tenure. In 1876, 44 Ph.D.'s were awarded in the country — among 25 universities. (The graduate enrollment in the country was only 198 in 1871; by 1890 it was 2,382; by 1910, 9,370; and in 1930, 47,255. 2,024 Ph.D.'s were awarded in 1930 by 74 universities.) With the growth in availability of persons with doctorates and under the influence of the University of Chicago, having a doctorate became the basic criterion for tenure by the early 1900s. The great research societies also developed at this time:

- the American Association for the Advancement of Science (1848)
- the American Medical Association (1847)
- the American Historical Association (1884)
- the Archeological Institute of America (1879)
- the American Psychological Association (1891)
- the American Chemical Society (1877)

Following the introduction of the requirement (or at least strong recommendation) that professors *publish** the results of their scholarly research — at Johns Hopkins and Chicago initially and then at all major universities — there developed a whole host of journals designed for this very purpose. Traditionally, America had no outlets for research publication. In Europe outlets were provided by the government as in France, by the professional societies as in England, or by the universities themselves as in Germany. In America the last two of these developed but not the first. Johns Hopkins first produced *The American Journal of Mathematics* in 1877 and soon thereafter it also had journals in the areas of chemistry, biology, physiology, psychology, and other areas. As indicated earlier, Chicago produced journals in geology, economics, astrophysics, sociology, theology, Hebrew (after all, William Rainey Harper was a Hebrew scholar), and the classics. Columbia introduced some 35 journals, and many other universities followed these examples and published journals in the areas in which they felt a major contribution could be made.

The professional societies, too, introduced journals — the American Philosophical Society in 1743, the American Academy of

---

*Frederick Rudolph, *The American College and University, A History,* (New York: Vintage Books [Random House], 1962).

Arts and Sciences in 1780, the American Association for the Advancement of Science (AAAS as it is popularly known), the American Chemical Society (ACS has just published its ten millionth *abstract* in its publication, *Chemical Abstracts*, designed to assist chemists in keeping up with a field that is growing exponentially), the Modern Language Association in 1883, the American Historical Association, the American Economic Association in 1885, the American Mathematical Society in 1888, and the Geological Society of America in 1888.

One of the divisions of the University of Chicago was its university press. Other universities, too, established publishing units which could produce books and monographs in addition to the university's journals. Johns Hopkins had a press by 1891, Columbia and California by 1893, and Yale, Harvard and Princeton followed suit very quickly. Again, most major universities have added a "press" to their organizations.

VIGNETTE

JAMES McKEEN CATTELL

Having earned a bachelor's degree from Lafayette College in 1880, Cattell studied at Johns Hopkins, earning the M.A. in 1883. He then went to Leipzig, where he received his Ph.D. in 1886, and he studied at Cambridge from 1886-1888. He became a lecturer at Yale and then filled the first chair of psychology at the University of Pennsylvania, having also taught at Bryn Mawr. He is known as the founder of experimental psychology mostly for his work at Columbia University, where he also founded the American Psychological Association. In addition to his work in psychology, Cattell was rather widely active; he was an anthropologist, he edited many diverse publications, including *American Men of Science*.

At Columbia, Cattell proved difficult to get along with. Nicholas Murray Butler recommended his retirement twice; the second time Cattell was involved in an incident regarding the faculty club. A Committee of nine (with John Dewey as a member) defended him, but he was, nevertheless, retired (fired) in 1917. In 1921 he was part of the founding of the Psychological Corporation, having had a major hand in the publication of journals that published scientific works — *Psychological Review, Science, Scientific Monthly, The American Naturalist,* and *School and Society.*

In the early history of graduate schools, the few students admitted were sort of self-selected as "superior and creative intellects." Growth in numbers, however, often resulted in the best minds moving toward the greatest rewards, the professions of medicine and law, and the researchers were often the less capable students. As numbers grew even larger, the need to have a doctor's degree to be competitive in various areas grew also. The goals were different, but the degree remained unchanged. It was thought that every student must concentrate upon one of the recognized specialities, which tended to become more and more narrow. Every student, before receiving the Ph.D., must make a contribution to knowledge. Partly as a means of self-defense against the inundation of subject-seekers, supervisors of dissertations fell back upon the tacit assumption that everything not known is worth knowing. The adoption of quantitative standards taken from the scientific disciplines by other fields whose best standards are qualitative made it possible to find an endless number of trivial objects of intellectual application upon which the dignified accolade "original contribution" could be bestowed. Dissertations abound on such subjects as the use of the comma in Shakespeare and the public opinion of Napoleon Bonaparte in Virginia.

Early colleges were really rather low-level institutions; the students were much younger than we are accustomed to in today's institutions and they had much less advance preparation. Graduating from colonial Harvard or Yale was probably akin to completing a good quality eight-grade school today. Most early colleges had attached to them or as actual parts of their structure preparatory schools. The University of Michigan was the first to adopt the system of admissions articulated with secondary schools. In 1870

Michigan began admission of students from selected schools which had been certified by the university as offering appropriate college admission studies. This paved the way for the Midwest development of the high school, which, of course, influenced the whole country. By 1870 most students in the Midwest were spending up to 16 years (of age) in the public schools. Under the movement begun by Michigan, the system developed into the popular eight-grade elementary school (which took youngsters about age six and retained them until about age 14) plus the four-grade high school (taking 14 year olds and keeping them until about age 18).

By 1872 Michigan, Minnesota, Iowa, and Wisconsin had developed high school certification programs. Indiana, Illinois, and Ohio followed quickly and by 1890 so did Texas, Missouri, and California. The acceptance into colleges of high school graduates (from certified high schools) had the additional effect (besides allowing larger numbers of students to aspire to college educations) of changing college admission requirements. The high schools were more responsive to local needs than other educational institutions and thus they tended to introduce the newer fields of study (sciences, modern languages, etc.) more quickly. This was done at the expense of some of the older studies (Greek and Latin, etc.), and so the graduates of these newer high schools were allowed to enter colleges on the strength of the certification of their schools without the traditional classical background.

Thus, the Midwestern state universities led in a movement that resulted in the major universities in this country becoming both more uniform in their requirements and standards and more democratic in the sense that they intended to serve a much broader population than was served in earlier times. It was in the period immediately following the Civil War that these changes rapidly took place.

In Germany the secondary schools had assumed the job of educating scholars to the point that they could enter into the upper division of a university (to use our modern-day terminology). That is, the freshman and sophomore years of college were actually covered in the secondary school so that the university took up at the upper division level and continued through the graduate levels, culminating with the award of the Ph.D. In part, this plan was desirable because it removed the adolescent student from the university setting and consequently removed from professors the burden of teaching such perhaps less motivated students relatively minor, routine, and uninteresting subject matter. G. Stanley Hall tried such a plan briefly at Clark University, and several private schools retained their students through what would be the thirteenth and fourteenth years before sending them on to a university.

William Rainey Harper of Chicago, Henry P. Tappan of Michigan, William Watts Folwell of Minnesota, and Daniel Coit Gilman of Johns Hopkins were among the leading educators who wanted the university to concentrate on higher level studies and research and so they pushed for the German-type arrangement. However, tradition in America had pretty firmly entrenched the 12 — 4 — + arrangement (12 years of public school, four years of college for a bachelor's degree, additional years of university work for advanced degrees). Harper introduced the idea of lower division and upper division classes at Chicago and he argued strongly for the inclusion of the lower division work in secondary schools. Actually, Harper proposed three different ways of establishing "junior colleges" (he also introduced this term into the vocabulary). First, a high school could simply add two years of study, making them equivalent to those of the colleges. Second, some of the less prominent four-year colleges could concentrate their efforts on the first two years of study and drop the upper division entirely; this would strengthen the weak colleges and aid the university as well. Third, new two-year colleges could be founded as needed to feed into the university. A few colleges followed plan two; as an example, Decatur Baptist College in Texas became a junior college in 1897 — its graduates went on to Baylor with advanced standing.* Joliet Junior College was established in 1902 (Joliet, Illinois) by separately organizing the thirteenth and fourteenth years of high school, and several others were also established in the Chicago area at this time.

In California Alexis F. Lange, dean of the University of California, and David Starr Jordan, president of Stanford, were leaders in

---

*William W. Brickman and Stanley Lehrer, *A Century of Higher Education*, (Westport, Connecticut: Greenwood Press, Publishers, 1962).

promotion of the idea that the junior college might serve two functions: replication of the lower division work of the university *and/or* provision of some advanced study for those less capable students who might never be able to attend the university. The latter was, of course, the beginning of the vocational training aspect of today's junior colleges. As this part of the program of junior colleges grew to approximately the same size as the alternate component, the colleges began to think of their mission in regard to their name. A movement began (and is today nearly complete) to change the name from junior college to *community college*.

Junior/community colleges spread most rapidly in those states that provided free or very low tuition for their students — California, Texas, Florida, Illinois — but their growth throughout the country has been phenomenal. By 1978* there were 1,193 public community colleges and 269 private ones; the enrollments were 3,873,000 and 155,000, respectively. We will hear of junior colleges once more in Chapter 8.

In 1931 John Henry Cardinal Newman wrote on *The Idea of a University* — as a place of teaching universal knowledge; having the purpose of making students into gentlemen; teaching force, comprehensiveness, command over one's powers, instinctive just estimate of things — not manners and habits. The function of the university is intellectual culture, not moral impression or mechanical production. The end of education is not accumulation of knowledge but mental enlargement. Thus, "smatterings" of knowledge in broad areas are not shallowness but enlargement. Knowledge is its own end. The university is an assemblage of men who respect and aid each other. This creates an atmosphere of thought which students "breathe." The student works within this intellectual tradition to comprehend the "great outlines" of knowledge. The content of university education should include the ideas, methods, orderliness, and principles of science; mathematics; grammar; chronology and geography; and

---

*Information taken from *The Condition of Education, 1980 Edition*. Published by the National Center for Education Statistics and produced by the U.S. Government Printing Office, Washington. D.C.

poetry. All subject matter is united and consists of acts and work of God. Thus, theology is a branch of knowledge and it impinges upon other branches. Teaching should be the formal introduction to the duties of life, but it should not be particularly utilitarian. Professional training is all right but not as the goal of a university education. Degrees should not be given on the basis of examinations but only following extensive intellectual intercourse on "every science under the sun." Self-education can do little for the mind; inter-human communication is essential.

James Bryant Conant, a distinguished organic chemist, was president of Harvard from 1933 to 1953. His studies of the American high school and of American colleges were scholarly and widely read. In his charge to the Harvard committee that studied college education, he said at the heart of a good citizenry was a good general education. He indicated that having the basic technical skills in mathematics and reading (and also in the sciences, as one might have expected) was not enough; what was also needed included history, art, literature, and philosophy — areas in which *information* is not the key element but *judgment* is. He wanted educated persons to have experienced right and wrong ethically as well as informationally. He also wanted general education to include values — "good taste" was a term used.

In the report of the Harvard Committee (1945), the need for a common ground, or unifying purpose, was expressed. The committee pointed to study of the great books of Western civilization as a way of discovering the intellectual forces that shaped the American way of thinking. The committee also suggested that it was appropriate to teach in American colleges an appreciation and understanding of American democracy without subjecting the study or the principles to the scrutiny of scientific investigation; in other words, it is the duty of colleges to pass on the culture and not to question it.

It was also suggested that an education should include an understanding, and acceptance, of the dignity of man and recognition of the duty of one man toward another. The common good rests in this individual acceptance and the individual good depends upon the common good. At the same time, the committee did not negate the importance of science. It pointed out that the questioning of the sciences results in the collection of empirical data and so knowledge becomes related to experience rather than only to abstract thinking; and it further pointed out that this is not out of keeping with the development of American traditions. Also, science in many of its applications has resulted in improvement of the human condition and so has worked toward, rather than away from, humanizing life. The conclusion of this discussion was that education must at the same time encourage acceptance of tradition and experimentation with change.

The committee report also insisted that both a general (i.e., liberal) education and a vocational education are appropriate. In spite of the fact that liberal education began under conditions in which only the privileged few were indeed free, it has the potential to enhance the freedom of all those who enjoy it. Thus, American education owes it to citizens to provide general education that all can partake of. An effective citizen must be able not only to work at a job to support himself and his dependents but also to apply his reasoning skills to the solution of general problems — problems that come to a vote or to the forum for discussion and resolution. Finally, it was urged that specialization in a field in which a person might ultimately find work and specialization in general education are, or ought to be, handled equivalently; each should consist of a series of integrated courses designed for the pupose of the overall outcome. General studies should not consist of the first course in each of the specializations taught for its specialists but of differently designed courses. Similarly, the liberal arts courses taken by, say, chemistry majors ought not to be just the first course for specialists in those liberal arts areas; these too should be part of the specially designed sequence of courses for general studies.

President Harry S. Truman in 1946 appointed a Commission on Higher Education (which, of course, became known as the Truman Commission) to investigate and report on the duties and responsibilities of the American system of higher education. The appointment of the commission was prompted by the large numbers of World War II veterans who were returning to college or entering college for the first time under federal support. The commission published a six-volume report on (1) goals, (2) expanding individual opportunities, (3) organization, (4) staffing, (5) financing, and (6) resource data.

In the report it was indicated that the number of students in colleges had been steadily increasing even before the influx of veterans, but that curriculum and equipment had been unable to keep pace with demands. The commission predicted that this problem would only grow worse. At the same time, the increasing technological complexity in America, particularly the advent of the atomic age, and the international nature of America's commitments were forecast to provide an impetus for even more stress on colleges and universities.

The report also emphasized the need for general education, speaking of the social role of education in a democracy, but it suggested (in contrast with the Harvard Report of only two years earlier) that the basis be in contemporary society rather than in history. The idea was that if American higher education was to educate citizens for this democracy, it should have a much clearer idea of the exact goals and problems within that democracy and it should provide instruction related to these.

The atomic bombs that had helped win the war were obviously prominent in the minds of the commission members. They pointed out the possibility of world catastrophe if atomic weapons (and also biological weapons) were not somehow restricted. It would become the duty of education to take the lead because decisions would ultimately be made by citizens (voters) and they must understand what they were dealing with. To aid in this type of education, the commission saw a need for American higher education to become involved in:

"Education for a fuller realization of democracy in every phase of living.

Education directly and explicitly for international understanding and cooperation.

Education for the application of creative imagination and trained intelligence to the solution of social problems and to the administration of public affairs."

The commission worried about the numbers of potential students who were not in college (in 1947 over two-thirds of the 18- and 19-year-old population were not in school) in spite of the pressures the system was facing from the numbers that were in college. It pointed out the three basic barriers — economic, curriculum, and personal (racial, religious, etc.). Rising tuition costs, along with general rising costs of living, prevented many from being able to go to college. The curricula in colleges were primarily academic and this tended to leave out those with "social sensitivity and versatility, artistic ability, motor skill and dexterity, and mechanical aptitude and ingenuity." The barriers to Negroes were specifically identified (segregation was lawful at the time in still about one-third of the states). It was concluded that "free and universal access to education, in terms of the interest, ability, and need of the student, must be a major goal in American education."

The goal above should be brought about, according to the Truman Commission, as follows.

1. High school education should be upgraded and made available to all normal youth.

2. Education through junior college should be provided free to all; free public schooling should be extended two years.

3. Scholarships should be available to those who need them in tenth through fourteenth grades — living-expense scholarships to offset the problem of financially burdened families.

4. Tuition charges in publicly supported colleges and universities should be lowered (in professional schools also), and for other institutions the problem should be alleviated through scholarships and fellowships.

5. Adult and continuing education should be taken on by colleges as part of their duty to the country and should be expanded.

6. All racial, sexual, religious, and other personal barriers should be removed from higher education.

Robert Maynard Hutchins wrote a reply to the report of the Truman Commission (published in *Educational Record*, April 1948) in which he called it "big and booming. It is confused, confusing, and contradictory. It has something for everybody. It is generous, ignoble, bold, timid, naive, and optimistic. It is filled with the spirit of universal brotherhood and the sense of American superiority. It has great faith in money. It has great faith in courses. It is antihumanistic and anti-intellectual. It is confident that vices can be turned into virtues by making them larger. Its heart is in the right place; its head does not work very well." Nevertheless, many recommendations of the Truman Commission were acted upon and many of its suggested changes have come to pass.

VIGNETTE

ROBERT MAYNARD HUTCHINS (1899-1977)

Hutchins was born in Brooklyn, New York but attended Oberlin College until the outbreak of World War I. During the war he served as an ambulance driver, then returned to Oberlin. He studied law at Yale and while there he became secretary of the corporation. Having earned his degree in law in 1925, he became acting dean and then dean of the school of law. In 1929, at the age of 30, he became president of the University of Chicago. Hutchins had become dissatisfied with the popular method of instruction in law: the case study method. He was also heavily influenced by the ideas of Mortimer Adler and the perennialist philosophy and came to the beliefs that the country's problems were based on: (a) the love of money, (b) a misconception of democracy, and (c) a misunderstanding of progress (he was opposed to vocationalism). At Chicago he instituted numerous reforms. One of these was a program under which high school juniors and seniors could enter the university, take these two years there, add another two years, and obtain a bachelor's degree at the end of this time. He established course credits instead of credit by examination, that is, one earned credit by completing a course rather than by passing a test. He proposed the "great books" curriculum, but it was not well accepted at Chicago; it was instituted at St. John's College for which institution Hutchins served as a trustee. He abolished athletics (competitive sports) at Chicago and, incidentally, allowed the Manhattan Project to operate in laboratories under the now-abandoned Stagg Field bleachers. Various of these reforms alienated alumni, faculty, and private donors so that by 1945 the university was in deep trouble. It had essentially lost its reputation as a seat of intellectual activity. Hutchins resigned the presidency and went to the

directorship of the Ford Foundation. There he continued his zest for reform by instituting a $15 million grant
for the study of democratic institutions (1954) in an effort to "save society."

In 1946 the Truman Commission report asked for a larger con-
ception of scholarship to include:

a. interpretive ability as well as research ability
b. skill in synthesis as well as in analysis
c. achievement in teaching as well as in investigation

By 1950, students in Ph.D. programs had the goal of college teaching on an average of about 65 percent (from a low of 34% in
chemistry to a high of 84% in English). Yet, Ph.D. degree programs
did little to prepare one for teaching and little to *broaden* knowledge.
(Knowledge was rather narrowed to the research speciality as I indicated earlier.) In addition, many Ph.D. students aspired to government service or industrial positions and for these two the programs
provided little preparation also.

Following 1946 the GI Bill introduced large numbers of students
into higher education, all practically oriented. The advent of the
space era (1956-Sputnik) brought still further practical emphasis on
the sciences, mathematics, and engineering. Yet, by 1958 a report
indicated that not much had changed since the report of the Truman
Commission, although there had been continued ferment over making graduate education more practical. Again, in 1962 it was reported that graduate schools had changed little since the nineteenth
century in organization, methods, and policies. It was said that:

a. In some universities graduate students had to wait several
   months to arrange for appointments with their advisors.
b. In the 12 most heavily federally supported universities, one-
   fifth of the faculty could greet few or no advanced graduate
   students by name.
c. At the big graduate schools (Berkeley, Columbia, Harvard,
   Yale), the Woodrow Wilson fellows reported less satisfaction
   with class size and with faculty guidance than those at other
   institutions.

In 1960 the Carnegie Commission had recommended:

a. a four-year limit for doctoral study
b. shorter dissertations
c. closer faculty supervision of graduate work
d. more flexible foreign language and examination requirements
e. teaching experience required as part of each doctoral program
f. a special two-year doctorate for college teachers (the doctor of arts)

Since 1965 the following have been noted:

a. more serious emphasis on the preparation of college teachers
b. greater breadth in graduate programs
c. less time spent in doctoral programs
d. emphasis on the significance of dissertations rather than on their novelty
e. redignified master's degree programs
   • 30 MAT (master of arts in teaching) programs
   • 40 special 3-year master's degree programs (where the junior and senior years and the next year of graduate study are merged)
   • numerous "advanced" or second master's degree programs
f. the idea of "publish or perish" giving way to searches for teacher-scholars
g. more honors and independent study programs
h. reduction, to an extent, of the fractionalization of the intellectual world
i. "super graduate schools" such as at Palo Alto and at Princeton and outside of universities

Remember that in its early history, education served one or both of the purposes: (1) to make one a learned person, hence a better citizen or a person more qualified to lead, or richer because of his unique skills, etc., or (2) to enable one to teach others in turn. Initially, the second of these led to "degrees" awarded by schools, the *licencia docendi* ("license to teach") and the *licencia docendi ubique* ("outstanding or special license to teach, or license to teach a very special subject" — the latter probably not intended in most cases). By the Renaissance, at least, the title "doctor" was also used to refer to those especially learned men who had devoted such extra effort to study that they were recognized as outstanding in their disputative and declamatory skills. Even prior to this (ca. A.D. 1000-1200), students who achieved the first level of knowledge, primarily in Latin, were called *bachelors* and those who had gone further and had successfully defended a "masterpiece" were called *masters*. The terms were also extended to professions other than teaching and the baccalaureate, the magister artium, and the doctor philosophiae became marks of acquisition of skills in many areas.

The American colonial colleges adopted the bachelor's and master's degrees from England, where, by 1636, the bachelor's degree was earned essentially by studying for four years and demonstrating certain required proficiencies, but the master's degree was acquired, not by adding new skills, but only by maturing three years beyond the bachelors and paying a continuing fee. At Harvard one could get a master's degree by keeping his name on the books of the college for three years beyond the bachelor's degree, paying $5, and "staying out of jail." The last such M.A. "in course" was awarded by Harvard in 1872; after that the M.A. was made an earned degree. (Yale awarded its first earned M.A. in 1876.)

Meanwhile, colleges had widely abused the awarding of honorary degrees. (Harvard took the lead, awarding three in 1692.) All degrees were used in this way, but the D.D. and the L.L.D. were the most widely awarded. (Over 200 different titles were used, including D.F.F., doctor of fortitude and faith.) The first honorary Ph.D. was given by Bushnell in 1852. In a few instances universities were incorporated for the sole purpose of awarding honorary degrees. By 1905 a master's degree could be (a) an honorary degree representing no training at all, (b) a degree given for in absentia study by the institution's own graduates, (c) a degree representing a year of genuine graduate study, or (d) a degree representing a year of additional undergraduate study beyond the B.A. Efforts were made to standardize the degree to represent true graduate-level study, but in

1932 the AAUP reported that this had not yet been accomplished, and in 1957 the American Association of Graduate Schools reported that the M.A. was still either a quick degree based on superficial performance or a consolation degree for those who couldn't do what was required to earn a Ph.D.

When Johns Hopkins opened it did not distinguish between the M.A. and Ph.D., but in 1909 it established the M.A. as the degree for college teachers and the Ph.D. as the degree for researchers. The M.A. was made a rigorous two-year degree (Yale followed suit in 1910). However, by that time the M.A. had become the standard badge of secondary school teachers and college teachers demanded the Ph.D. The doctorate remained a double-purpose degree: college teaching and research. The emphasis in degree programs was on the latter, but by far the more usual outcome was the former. Johns Hopkins took the lead in defining the Ph.D. as a research degree; it was the first institution also to require publication of the dissertation (1887).

In 1920 Harvard introduced the Ed.D. as a doctoral-level degree for practicing educators. It was widely adopted and "became as confused as the Ph.D." The D.A. (doctor of arts) was proposed in 1960 and endorsed in 1970 by the Carnegie Commission on Higher Education. This degree too was abused, particularly on the "dissertation" requirement, and doctorates were based on books of poems, novels, and even on musical compositions. It has been effectively dropped with degrees such as the M.F.A., the M.B.A., and advanced M.A. replacing it.

CHAPTER 5

THE ELECTIVE SYSTEM

FROM 1636 forward nearly 200 years American colleges and universities had essentially fixed curricula. The major purpose of education was to train an elite citizenry and (very early) to train ministers and it was felt that the way to do this was "known." However, with the increase of secularization and with the introduction of vocationalism into the colleges, the fixed curriculum became less and less operable. Thomas Jefferson introduced some choice into the curriculum at William and Mary in 1779, but at the University of Virginia (1825) there was more choice. Actually, as I said earlier, it was a choice among the eight schools available, ancient languages, modern languages, mathematics, natural philosophy, natural history, anatomy and medicine, moral philosophy, and law. There were no electives within a school, but the student who did not seek a degree could take any courses he chose.

George Ticknor, a friend of Jefferson's, proposed a similar structure for Harvard in 1825. Upperclass students were allowed limited electives, students could advance as rapidly as they were able, and non-degree students could take a "partial course." The idea of parallel courses (programs) and partial courses was copied in many institutions after 1825.

VIGNETTE

GEORGE TICKNOR (1791-1871)

Ticknor attended Dartmouth and graduated at age

111

16. He then read law (that was, and to an extent still is, the expression used to describe studying law, perhaps because of the extensive use of the case study method) for three years and followed this with a tour of the United States and Canada, finally travelling to Europe. He found the English universities unimpressive, but he paused for study at Goettingen and in Italy, France, and Spain. He was greatly impressed with the German *lehrfreiheit*, saying in a letter in 1815, "If truth is to be attained by freedom of inquiry, as I doubt not it is, the German professors and literati are certainly in the high road, and have the way quietly open before them...."*

Ticknor had been married just before beginning his trip to Europe to a vivacious, intellectual young lady and she, no doubt, had a considerable influence on his thinking about higher education.

Harvard wanted Ticknor badly enough as a professor that they held a position open for him for three years while he was abroad. He returned to this position, the Smith Professorship of French and Spanish Languages, a position he held until 1835. He became known as a good lecturer but distant personally; as a matter of fact, it was Ticknor who popularized the lecture method at Harvard. (Ticknor was immediately succeeded in the indicated professorship by Henry Wadsworth Longfellow and he, in turn, by James Russell Lowell — a most eminent trio.) Ticknor stated that Harvard had been operating since its opening as though it were a very small school with every student having to be taught by every professor in very small groups if not individually. And this was despite the fact that at the time Harvard had over 300 students and 20 or more instructors. He argued that the amount and quality of time spent by each professor with each student had been reduced so that the system was merely one of testing superficial knowledge rather than one of examining topics in depth. He also said that Harvard was neither a university nor a "respectable high school" (meaning a preparatory school for professional schools, not what we think of as high schools today).

He was also known for his concerns with curricular reforms and for his support of academic freedom. The

---

*Quoted from Item 2. Part IV. In Richard Hofstadter and Wilson Smith (Eds.): *American Higher Education: A Documentary History*, (Chicago: University of Chicago Press, 1961).

latter stemmed from his belief in the efficacy of the German system. In the case of the former he proposed a division of the university into departments, an arrangement that had not been tried in this country before. His ideas were rejected, and Ticknor left Harvard in 1835. While there, however, he was successful in upgrading the Boston Public Library (libraries had become a special interest of his, and he lamented the unusability of Harvard's library) and developing it as a center for literary research.

VIGNETTE

EDWARD EVERETT (1794-1865)

As a young man Everett was precocious, entering Harvard at age 13 (the youngest of 49 students in his class) and graduating at 17. He had studied at Exeter where his older brother, a Harvard graduate, was a teacher. He was apparently sort of restless; he entered the ministry but dropped this job to travel in Europe. There, he earned his Ph.D., the first to be awarded to an American by the University of Goettingen. He joined the Harvard faculty and became president of the university in 1846. While at Harvard he gave a "famous" lecture on George Washington 129 times and donated the fees to the Mount Vernon Ladies' Society that was to be used in purchasing Mount Vernon. (He also gave a two-hour speech preceding Lincoln's address at Gettysburg.)

He resigned the Harvard presidency after only three years, spent three years with his family, and was appointed to fill the term of Daniel Webster as secretary of state under Millard Filmore. (He was a friend of Webster's.) He served in the senate but resigned this position, also. He did complete four terms as governor of Massachusetts.

In 1871 Noah Porter, conservative president of Yale, rejected the elective system, saying that students had neither the maturity nor the information needed to make the judgments required. The Yale Report of 1828 had presented a defense of the traditional system and suggested that the proper curriculum was a "thorough study of the ancient languages." This report did not reject advanced (graduate) study with electives, but it did maintain that the undergraduate curriculum should be traditional, fixed, and "liberal." Yale was not a mover in the development of the elective system in this country.

VIGNETTE

NOAH PORTER (1811-1892)

> Porter studied at Yale, obtained the B.A. in 1831, the M.A. in 1836, and was ordained a minister. He became president of his alma mater in 1871 and remained until 1886. During his term the school of law and the school of medicine were both reorganized, but the factor for which Porter is best known is his resistance to change. He favored texts and recitations. He retained the segregation of the sexes. He opposed electives. Under his presidency, Yale grew and prospered.

Francis Wayland, president of Brown, published a book in 1842 proposing a much broadened curriculum. In 1850 he persuaded the Brown University Corporation to adopt an elective system which included a "partial course" and a kind of extension program. He also instituted a Ph.B. degree and a master's degree available after only four years of study. The quality of students declined and enrollments at first jumped and then fell off; Wayland resigned and Brown reverted to a more conservative program.

Henry Tappan also tried to introduce electives at Michigan both as parallel courses and (in 1885) as choices within a program — only for seniors, however. Tappan fought for these programs for 12 years, but in 1863 he was dismissed from Michigan without seeing them come into use.

It was Charles William Eliot at Harvard who really brought the elective system to prominence. He was chosen president of Harvard in 1869, over the objections of the overseers, and remained for 40 years. He wanted three things in his program:

1. freedom of choice in studies
2. opportunity to win academic distinction in single subjects or in special lines of study
3. a discipline which imposes on the individual the responsibility for his own conduct (including his learning).

He reported on this in 1885 in a speech that was published three years later. By 1874 Harvard had a required curriculum only for freshmen, although rhetoric, philosophy, history, and political science were required also at higher levels. The only restriction on electives was that sequence had to be observed — elementary courses first, advanced courses later. By 1895 the only remaining required courses for freshmen were two in English and one in a modern foreign language. The change was gradual; Eliot (although a chemist) was diplomatic but persistent. He attacked faculty psychology and defended psychology of individual differences. And he used the elective struggle as a vehicle for bringing the new areas of science into equality with older established disciplines.

The electives that could be chosen by freshmen students at Harvard were limited to about 20% of the available undergraduate courses. All freshmen had to take English, and either French or German, and they were not allowed to take more than two courses in any one subject. In many cases the student had to satisfy the professor that he was capable of doing the work required in a course before he was admitted, and in any case an advisor had to approve a student's choice of electives before registration. For freshmen the system was not as "free" as one might have been led to believe. For all students the courses offered were divided into 14 "examination groups," and no student was allowed to take two courses from the same group at any one time. (Freshmen took five courses; sophomores, juniors, and seniors took four.)

The Harvard elective system amounted to social Darwinism in which the ablest who chose wisely "survived." And this was true of areas as well as of students, and also of subjects, couses, and even of professors.

The Harvard faculty appointed a committee in 1902 to study the elective system as it had developed there, and in 1904 this committee reported that it had found the system too lenient. Students were taking classes haphazardly, or because they were easy or conveniently scheduled, and they were doing less preparation than in the past. Changes were recommended, but these were not made until after A. Lawrence Lowell succeeded Eliot as president in 1909. Lowell changed the system to one of "concentration and distribution" rather than free electives as had been the case. Of 16 full-year courses, 6 had to be concentrated in one major field, 6 more in three other fields, and only 4 were left elective.

Meanwhile, Princeton, under James McCosh, had resisted the elective system (at least *free* electives), relying on faculty psychology for the reason. McCosh distrusted students, saying that they would take the easy way to a degree if given the chance. Also, being a Calvinist, McCosh felt that most men could not be trusted to know what was right for them; he believed in an elite authoritarian system and he was suspicious of the new science and of the changes it was bringing into the colleges.

The curricular laissez faire era extended from about 1870 until 1910. There were essentially four systems: ·

1. total election
2. about half fixed, half elective
3. major-minor
4. group system, with little choice within a group (science, history, etc.) but choices among groups

Cornell went elective, as did Columbia, William and Mary, and Stanford. In 1901 a survey found 35% of the colleges mostly elective, 12% about half elective, and 53% less than half elective. Colleges in the Midwest and West tended to be elective, those in the South and in New England the least elective; women's colleges were marginal.

In a recent study, eight major universities listed from a minimum of 2,469 courses to a maximum of 5,975. One college had more courses than it had students. In 1636 Harvard's first class of 9 students took 10 subjects, the same for all 9 students. And the first president of Harvard taught all of these courses. Today over a half million professors in this country teach over 2 million classes to about 10 million students in about 3,000 institutions for some 1,500 separate degrees.

One can identify three curriculum eras and several sub-eras:

1. 1636-1870 — Classical
2. 1870-1960 — Industrial-Professional
   a. 1870-1910 — Free electives in rapid development
   b. immediately following 1862 — Development of mechanical arts and agriculture in curricula
   c. with the growth of universities — Development of departmentalization
3. 1960-present — Consumer oriented

One can also point to major additions to curriculum:

Eighteenth century — Physical sciences
Nineteenth century — Modern languages
Twentieth century — Social and behavioral sciences
Last 100 years — New professions

A classical education was useful to clergymen, teachers, doctors, and lawyers in colonial days, but its basic problem was that the curriculum was essentially controlled by ministers. It represented the high culture of the era as seen by the clergy and passage through the curriculum served to identify members of the "educated" class. The industrial and professional era was characterized by the production of new knowledge, new technology, and human capital (i.e., new professionals). There was a de-emphasis on culture in the curriculum and an emphasis on useful knowledge and employment. The requirements for a major set the pattern for curriculum and these were influenced by manpower needs. In the consumer era there was more time for electives and there were more courses in the arts; more courses for non-majors in various fields; more part-time, extension, and evening courses; and more community service courses.

By 1900 the following could describe American higher education:

1. broad elective curricula
2. modern subjects — languages, sciences, social sciences — included in liberal arts
3. skills courses
4. universities replacing colleges
5. specialization for professions began to encroach upon the liberal arts
6. individual differences recognized

7. secular preparation essentially replacing religious preparation

8. greater freedom for students, socially as well as in curriculum

9. often the appeal of a college was by means of "prominent scholars" since programs were so varied

10. all levels of society began to aspire to college degrees.

VIGNETTE

ABRAHAM FLEXNER (1866-1959)

In 1910 Flexner reported on a survey of medical schools in the United States and Canada and he suggested that of the 154 schools surveyed, 120 should be closed because their training was poor or low level, because their students were not even required to have high school diplomas for admission, and the like. A graduate of Johns Hopkins and of Harvard, Flexner ran his own secondary school. He was generally a critic of American higher education, saying that universities should advance knowledge through non-utilitarian research and that graduate schools should be separated from the arts and sciences and liberal arts schools. He was also opposed to the elective system. He founded the Institute for Advanced Study at Princeton in 1930.

In most colleges and universities today, electives are considerably more limited than they were at the apex of the elective system at Harvard under Eliot. In general studies (or liberal studies, or other similarly titled segments of degree programs), the electives are usually allowed as choices of courses within groupings. At my own institution one is required to take eighteen hours of languages and cultures, nine hours of sciences and mathematics, and fifteen hours of social sciences, and there are both area specifications in each of these and in some cases specific course lists from which one must choose. There are also some limitations of choices determined by the major which will be pursued later. Most colleges do follow a major-minor type of program also, and in these the choice of the major and the minor are, of course, elective except that certain majors might implicitly require specific minors (mathematics for the physical sciences, for example). Course electives are allowed within the major and minor, but these are usually quite limited, a specific set and sequence of courses being more the pattern.

Since most bachelor's degree programs require somewhere in the neighborhood of 120 semester hours of credit, and since the general studies component is frequently about one-third of this and the major may be from 45 to 60 hours and the minor may be from 20 to 24 hours, there may be some "free electives" left in many degree programs. Some students may be able to take advantage of this to sample other areas of study or to broaden their acquaintance with the fields of knowledge; others may find that their needs for certification or licensing (in order to be able to obtain a job as a result of their college education) practically demand that they take certain courses or course sequences so that they end up with no electives.

At the same time, colleges today do not limit students to taking the specified number of credits for a degree. A student who desires to take advantage of the "elective system" may take as many courses as he/she wants as long as the prerequisites are met and as long as they are not required to fit into a specific degree program.

CHAPTER 6

PSYCHOLOGIES AND PHILOSOPHIES

IN old Greece and ancient Rome the wealthy ruling class was the educated class. Education was basically for either of two purposes: (1) to rule or (2) just to be educated. To be sure, there was some utilitarian education, such as reading and writing and mathematics (keeping accounts), but these were for slaves, not for the "educated" individuals. During the college period in Europe, education was still for an elite, but this elitist education was more utilitarian than before. The basic purpose was to make a man a good clergyman, a good teacher, or good in the business world. However, the apprenticeship was still the way most people learned trades and colleges were for the richer, the more professional, the elite. European universities, when they developed, were not totally different from the colleges, but they did add to their basic purpose the finding of new knowledge. (It was this that set them aside as universities rather than colleges.) Also, it may have been more likely that a university graduate was considered "learned" than a college graduate — after all, one could become a *doctor* through university study.

As we have seen, the first American colleges had as their basic function the preparation of clergymen, but a second purpose was liberal education. This included the training of "gentlemen" (remember the fellow commoners) and "educating the whole man." It also included, in somewhat later curricula, the idea that a college man should learn to learn, that is, to continue to educate himself. (Cardinal Newman, of course, did not espouse this idea, but it was in early curricula nevertheless.) In still later curricula the idea of humanism, the development of an individual to his peak of "worth,"

120

was emphasized. All of these fit well with the extant psychology of the time, faculty psychology or the training of the mental faculties by practice.

With the introduction into college curricula of practical subjects, the purposes of higher education changed greatly and could be characterized in terms of:

    a. vocational training, training for a more or less specific job or vocation

    b. specific agricultural and/or mechanical training

    c. general pragmatic education, the acquisition of general skills that would fit one to do a variety of types of jobs

    d. development of scholars (researchers) who would discover new knowledge.

The levels of education might be described in terms of these modes of knowing:

    a. (elementary school) inspired information

    b. (secondary school and college) uncovered facts

    c. (college and graduate school) discovered principles

    d. (graduate school) invented theories

    e. (self-acquisition) values and aesthetics

But a look at the curricula of colleges and universities in our history will suggest that American higher education has itself gone through this set of modes of knowing. The early colonial colleges dealt purely with inspired information, for example, and it was not a purpose of higher education to invent theories until the development of the graduate schools and the true universities.

Three trends can be identified in American higher education:

    1. from religious education to secular education (In colonial Harvard and Yale some 70% of graduates went into the ministry; by 1810 it was only 10%.)

    2. from an elite student body to a popular student body (Changes have been seen from educating gentlemen to educating scholars, to preparation for vocations, to life training.)

    3. from general curricula to specialized curricula.

Paralleling these trends, but more elaborate in their changes, were the following teaching procedures seen in evolution in this list.

1. dialog between a teacher and one or more learners
2. lecture (The teacher spoke; the learner wrote for later study.)
3. disputation and declamation
    a. seminars (which developed out of these)
    b. colloquia
    c. recitation
4. laboratory (introduced in the nineteenth century in the sciences, it spread into other fields)
    a. demonstration by professor
    b. demonstration by student
    c. use of "unknowns" (The professor knew what was being sought, but the learner did not.)
    d. true investigation by students as well as by professors
5. honors programs (Introduced at Swarthmore around 1920)
6. theses
    a. graduate level (The peak developed at Johns Hopkins as we have seen.)
    b. undergraduate level (Some small colleges have followed a curriculum that mimics graduate school and requires undergraduates to carry out an investigation and write a thesis.)
7. "Great books" and the like (curricula that assume that the greatest source of knowledge is in the writings of great minds of the past)
8. cooperative learning (various work-study programs)
9. technology and individualization (epitomized in current settings by computer-assisted instruction programs and by various "modular" plans for the instruction of individual students)
10. teaching and research (the idea that research and teaching are complements of each other and not dichotomies in university life)
11. teaching exemplars (the professor teaches not only by what he says but also by his example)
12. competency-based education (the idea that what is important for the student is the acquisition of a set of competen-

cies and that it does not matter how these competencies are learned).

Again, in parallel with these teaching procedures, one can identify a set of teaching models that are tied with either a philosophy or a psychology in many cases.

a. The *Socratic Model* had as its primary object inquiry, the development of skill in questioning. The method was dialetic (conversation) and inductive reasoning (generalization from numerous experiences). The modern-day equivalent is, perhaps, discovery learning or possibly concept learning.

b. The *Jesuit Model*, sometimes referred to as classical humanism, had the goal of acquiring skills in speaking, writing, reasoning, and criticizing. The process was to master Latin, Greek, logic, natural and moral philosophy, metaphysics, theology, and sacred scripture (all materials with built-in values). The method included prelection (public discourse), disputation, review, rivalry, and rote learning. In review, the student recited what he had learned before the professor and was later tested over the same material — not an uncommon procedure today. In rivalry, the goal was for students to "trip" one another and to catch errors made in presentations — another procedure that is not uncommon today, particularly in professional meetings.

c. Goals of the *Personal Development Model* were the acquisition of occupational skills, the development of a good personality, the discovery of talents, the growth of a positive self-image, and development of the ability to relate to one's fellow man. Teaching procedures involved careful pacing of experiences to assure success and pride in achievement, no drill, and de-emphasis on specific content (with the exception of selected occupational skills).

d. An *Individualized Model*, which can be based on proposals of William Glaser (1962), included the procedure diagrammed in Figure 1.
A computer education procedure developed by Lawrence Stolurow, the teaching plans published by Robert Gagne, and various other plans detailing instructional procedures

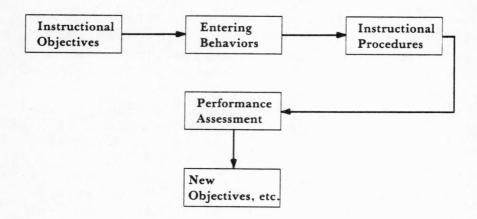

Figure 1. An individualized model.

seem to fit this model. The idea is to state the objectives of instruction, to identify those skills that the learner already possesses with respect to these objectives, and then to prepare instructional procedures to build upon these skills. Performance assessment involves matching learner skills against instructional objectives; when there is an adequate match, the learner moves on to a new set of objectives and the process is repeated.

e. A *Thinking Model* can be described in relation to what is sometimes called problem solving, or discovery learning, or creativity (perhaps associated with the psychologies of Jerome Bruner, Jean Piaget, and Jean Guilford and with the ideas on creativity of E. Paul Torrance.

f. Finally, the *Competency-Based Instruction Model* is the base for programed instruction, either by book or by machine or computer. It is also the base for some large-scale programs for the development of specific competencies through a variety of procedures; the important thing in these programs is the development of the competencies, not the procedures through which they are acquired.

Along with the above models, there can also be described a set of teacher models; as a matter of fact, various writers in the past have described such models in several different ways. According to Henry Canby (1890-1920), teachers fit into five patterns:

a. hard-boiled (I have the information, come and get it.)
b. indifferent (little attention paid to students as people or even as learners)
c. factual (Since the basis of learning is the acquisition of information, students "cramming" to pass tests is strongly associated with this teacher model.)
d. enthusiastic (interesting classes)
e. idealistic (lots of questioning and discussion of values)

Joseph Axelrod has proposed a different taxonomy of teacher types:

a. drillmaster
b. content-centered
c. instructor-centered
d. intellect-centered
e. person-centered

The characteristics of these five teacher types are as follows:

The Drillmaster —

- encourages quick automatic responses to questions
- is the ultimate authority in the class
- allows only one correct answer
- uses repetition rather than reinforcement
- emphasizes skills and specific items of knowledge as desired outcomes of instruction

The Content-Centered Teacher —

- believes in "covering" the prescribed material
- knows just what content is needed, its sequences, and the entering and leaving skills of learners
- does not accept "alternate styles" of teaching-learning
- believes that as he is there to teach, the student is there to learn
- sees all students as alike
- considers joint inquiry nonsense
- prefers an emotion-free classroom
- is cool, rational, scholarly, and non-involved with students

The Instructor-Centered Teacher —
- plays the role of model in the classroom
- believes that what the teacher does is more important than subject-matter content
- wants learners to imitate the teacher's behavior rather than to acquire a given set of information
- sees knowledge as process
- is central to all class activity
- may be a "showman," have charisma, and be warm in interpersonal relationships outside of class

The Intellect-Centered Teacher —
- strongly believes in knowledge as process (condemns knowledge-as-product teaching)
- concentrates on rational activity — the how and why of knowledge rather than the what
- uses analysis and problem solving as teaching techniques; concentrates on modes of doing these rather than on a given set of content
- may examine progress by presenting new situations and requiring students to analyze them

The Person-Centered Teacher —
- believes that intellectual development and other personality development cannot be separated
- maintains that self-development (achieving an appropriate level of humanness) is the real goal of learning
- teaches by issuing challenges to solve problems using skills not already available to the learner
- would never use drill, rote learning, patterning, and the like as teaching techniques

The Undecided Teacher (one who does not totally fit any of these five categories) —
- has some of the characteristics of each of the other types
- is not consistent in his feelings regarding teaching and instructional modes; one time feels a given way, another time may feel the exact opposite
- has heard about each of the other types of teacher and from time to time would like to emulate each of them

According to Kenneth Boulding, one can think of professors in terms of dichotomies as follows:

  a. social superior versus social equal
  b. authority versus co-learner
  c. hostile versus encouraging
  d. enthusiastic and sure of relevance versus apathetic and unsure
  e. master of skills versus servant of skills
  f. cooperative with other areas versus jealous and reclusive
  g. self-dignified and recognizes dignity of others versus not so

Learning psychologies that have had influence upon college teaching can be identified as:

  a. stimulus-response
  b. Gestalt
  c. "modern" developmental ideas (Bruner, Piaget)
  d. neuropsychological ideas (Hebb)
  e. "new" stimulus-response (Skinner)

Philosophies that have had major influence upon college teaching are:

  a. faculty "psychology"
  b. experimentalism (related to theoretical instruction)
  c. humanism (relevance)
  d. reconstructionism

With these listed as background, one can look at specific educational "theories" (placed in quotes because I do not believe that these are theories in the scientific sense but only paradigms or models).

1. Formal Discipline
  a. Scholastic realism (Aristotle)
     Form and matter (i.e., soul and substance) are in everything.
  b. Stimulus-response and Christianity (St. Thomas Aquinas)
     Knowing involves assimilation of forms and integration with man's rational form (soul).
  c. Seventeenth century dualism (Descartes)
     The world is matter only, man has a mind. Much learning is innate (in the mind) although mind and body are separate and distinct.

d. Classical empiricism (John Locke)
   All ideas ever found in the mind derive from sensation or introspection.

These models, all listed under Formal Discipline, led to the teaching ideas of "faculty psychology" under which it was believed that the way to become educated was to exercise the faculties of the mind in the same way that one becomes physically strong by exercising the muscles. To this basic and pervasive idea over a long period of time, Locke added the need for direct experiences in learning — at least in some types of learning.

2. Natural Perfection

Rousseau expressed the idea that the roots of good are in the universe and that man was made to do good, although he is free to do evil. Thus, education should develop the good by selecting only those subjects, that content, and those experiences that will lead to good.

3. Apperception

According to Herbart (1893), what has already been learned influences what can be learned. All mental activities can be accounted for by the laws of association. Under this belief the aims of education should be empirical, speculative, aesthetic, sympathetic, social, and religious. Teaching would involve recitation consisting of five parts: (1) preparation (developing the mind), (2) presentation, (3) comparison, (4) generalization, and (5) application.

4. Habit Tendency

William James (*Talks to Teachers*, 1889) said that learning is developing habits and tendencies toward behaviors. Mind is a stream of thought, no thought ever recurring exactly as before. Knowledge is by acquaintance (a sort of accumulation) or by use (in which one thinks, feels, and operates with the information).

5. Human Wants

Edward Thorndike (ca. 1930) said that the goals of education are to prepare learners to meet the needs of "the good life." The learning process consists of conditioning.

6. Universal Growth (Progressivism)

John Dewey (ca. 1916) published his ideas on learning and these had a heavy influence on public schools, although they were somewhat less accepted by colleges.

7. Self-Realization

Track 1 — Humanism (Piaget)

Track 2 — Behavior modification (Skinner)

The sequence of changes in models for college teaching was:

a. mental discipline
b. vocationalism (still including the procedures of mental discipline)
c. transfer (including vocationalism)
d. pragmatism (solving daily problems)
e. humanism (lift humanity through education)
f. rationalism (Hutchins and Adler; the "great books" approach to college teaching, learning for its own sake)
g. re-emphasis on pragmatism (the Dewey era)
h. reconstructionism (George Counts proposed that learning should be value-free and that the real purpose of higher education should be to improve the society through questioning its current procedures and institutions.)
i. re-emphasis on humanism (fairly recent, with the psychology of Piaget coming into use at the college level)
j. "back to basics"

The colonial colleges and many of their immediate followers were openly elitist;* as a matter of fact, it was not until the secularization of colleges had been completed that the "common man" could actually find an appropriate college program to meet his needs. Of course, Brown had opened with the goal of admitting anyone who could benefit from its course of study, but this still meant a rather elite type of student since the classical course of study was very demanding. Virginia had an elective system, but remember that it was truly elective only for non-degree students and it was still not as practical as Jefferson might have wanted it to be. Cornell, the first of

*Frederick Rudolph. *The American College and University. A History,* (New York: Vintage Books [Random House]. 1962).

the A & Ms, was truly practical and paved the way for the admission into colleges of "ordinary folk." And then the state universities and later the junior colleges further opened the door of higher education. A result of this door opening was the development of the idea that the average student was somehow superior to those more able — a sort of anti-elitist attitude.

Swarthmore was a leader in counteracting this attitude; an honors program was introduced in 1922. Both Princeton, under President Woodrow Wilson, and Harvard, under President Abbott Lawrence Lowell, introduced the preceptor system and tutorials. Reed College in Portland, Oregon (1912) required a senior thesis and it still does. Columbia had a "general honors" program consisting of study of the great books.

Berea College (Kentucky) provided employment for those students who would otherwise be unable to attend. However, by 1906 this resulted in there being two distinct groups of students at the college: those who had to work and those who could pay their own way and did not have to work. Fearing the undesirable consequences of this dichotomy, the trustees established the policy that today requires all students at the college to work. The work requirement may be met in college departments, in jobs such as janitor or security police, in student industries, or by working in surrounding communities. Payment for this work is credited against the cost of education in lieu of tuition payments.

In 1906 the University of Cincinnati introduced a cooperative work study program for engineering students in which alternating periods of study and work were used. This pattern was copied by Northeastern University (Boston), where it became the largest such program in the country.

John Dewey published *Democracy and Education* in 1916 and it had a relatively immediate effect upon public school practices. The colleges were a bit slower to take up the ideas of Dewey, but the depression years in America provided a climate in which this did occur.* Programs called "core courses" were introduced; studies called

---

*Frederick Rudolph. *The American College and University, A History.* (New York: Vintage Books [Random House]. 1962).

American Civilization, American Studies, or American Culture attempted to integrate information from several areas of traditional study into applications toward the solution of real problems (a la Dewey). The movement was known as progressive education, and it appeared to result in a watering down of the traditional instruction in the disciplines to the point where a smattering of information was all right as long as it could be applied to some everyday problem. The departure from tradition went even farther than had the elective system of Eliot.

Variations of the Dewey-inspired systems were tried. Antioch College opened in 1921 with a program integrating liberal arts education with work experience. Students alternated periods of study on campus and work in the community over a five-year period. Antioch was also run in a democratic fashion, with decisions made jointly by students and professors. Hiram College (Hiram, Ohio, 1849) introduced in 1934 an intensive course system. Bennington College (Bennington, Vermont, 1932) attempted to integrate the curriculum and the extracurriculum, work and play, classroom and experience. It also varied from tradition by employing professors not for their academic credentials but for their life experiences.

Alexander Meiklejohn devised a program at Wisconsin in 1928 that was aimed at increasing the motivation of students for study. The philosophical idea was that by increasing the possibilities for interaction among students and instructors, encouraging informality, and presenting liberal arts subjects in such a way as to make them appear applicable to the ordinary student, motivation would be increased. In practice, Wisconsin did the first of these and the second, but when it came to the third, the program appeared rather traditional. In the first year the course of study was the Athens of Pericles and Plato, in the second year Modern America. The idea did not work as it had been envisioned by Meiklejohn.

Still another experimenter of note was Robert Maynard Hutchins at Chicago. However, his reforms were proposed to abolish the emphases on evolution, on empirical evidence, on progressivism in general and on vocationalism in particular, and on anti-intellectualism. Hutchins said that the university had moved from its intended purposes and ought to return to the classical curriculum, not to that of Yale circa 1828, but rather to a curriculum consisting of study of the great books.

VIGNETTE

ALEXANDER MEIKLEJOHN (1872-1964)

Meiklejohn was born in England and came to the United States at the age of eight. He was educated in the Rhode Island public schools and earned the B.A. and M.A. from Brown University; his Ph.D. was from Cornell. He was quite athletic and considered making this into a career, but his intellectual activities won over. In 1963 he received the Medal of Freedom from then U.S. President Lyndon B. Johnson on the basis of (a) his attempts to abolish the House Committee on Un-American Activities, (b) his activities in the American Civil Liberties Union and other civil rights groups, and (c) his strong insistence that loyalty oaths were unconstitutional.

His ideas were always considered a bit "offbeat." He taught philosophy at Brown and then became president of Amherst College. At Amherst he employed Robert Frost and similar specialists and "thinkers" who did not have college degrees but, he felt, could serve the students in exceptional ways as instructors. He proposed a new kind of college and was eventually invited to install this plan at Wisconsin in 1926. Known as the Wisconsin Experiment, the first year of study was to be spent learning about the culture of ancient Athens and the second year about American civilization. Faculty and students were to "learn together" as in the old days when professors and students alike were known as scholars and were not particularly distinguished from one another. Meiklejohn felt that every person should be allowed to express his beliefs and that the way to combat such problems as communism (remember the era in which he lived) was to "hear them out" rather than to try to suppress them. He said that freedom of speech really means freedom of mind. And he got into a literary duel with Sidney Hook over the question of whether or not communists should be allowed to teach in America.

In a basically non-liberal time, Meiklejohn's ideas were not totally accepted. The Wisconsin Experiment failed to work out and he was asked to leave the university under the "charges" that he favored communism and "free love."

From a list given earlier in this chapter, one would infer that the psychology (or philosophy) of today's colleges is tied to the "back-to-basics" idea. This is probably true. The major teaching procedure in today's colleges is probably lecture or lecture-discussion. Laboratories are still heavily used, at least in the sciences and art, and simulations are still found good in business fields, but these might actually be considered a part of the "basics" in these areas. The individualized programs of a few years ago, the "Keller Plan," the Postlethwaite "Audio-Tutorial" plan, and others, are not widely used anymore. The "multimedia" programs of instruction either have not developed as they were expected to do or have been cut back from peaks reached some years ago. Competency-based programs once served as the foundation of whole colleges or at least of whole licensing programs. These have given way to modified programs, at most, in which the mode of achieving the specified competencies is more traditional than it was for a time in our history.

Most college students sit in lecture halls or smaller classrooms and take notes while their professors attempt to impart knowledge. Most use libraries extensively to read, not the great books espoused by Hutchins, but more recent and more practical books on the reading lists provided by their professors. Most students produce papers and take tests and are graded by comparison either with a preset standard of achievement or with the performance of their peers; the criterion-referenced testing that went with many of the individualized programs and with the competency-based programs has not become widely popular.

An innovation that *is* being introduced involves computers. Of course, CAI (computer-assisted instruction) was introduced in the same era as the multimedia programs, but the more recent development of personal home computers has caused the country to become so computer-conscious that universities almost have to include computers in their programs in some way. Computer laboratories are common. Computer instruction is being developed to a greater extent than ever before. And students can "major" in computer work in several different ways. However, the whole computer movement may simply be a part of the "back to basics" effort, since computers are an unavoidable part of everyday life in this country.

CHAPTER 7

ACADEMIC FREEDOM

PLATO claimed that a scholar must be able to follow an argument "whithersoever it may lead." And this ideal, with ups and downs, grew to the freedom of both students and professors in the German universities described as *lehrfreiheit* and *lernfreiheit*. Some of the history of this development follows.

In A.D. 1158 Emperor Frederick Barbarossa issued an edict promising scholars safe conduct, protection at home, and compensation for any unlawful injury. While one may wonder at the conditions that led to the need for such an edict, the edict itself was perhaps the first step in the direction of guaranteeing scholars that their scholarship would not lead to retribution. In 1219 the Bishop of Paris was forbidden to excommunicate a master or a student without express permission from the pope, again an apparent violation of academic freedom but one that was held in check. In 1361 the King of France freed a scholar who had been imprisoned on heresy charges, a truly forward move for that day and time. By the early sixteenth century both the University of Paris and Oxford University had developed a sort of self-policing procedure among scholars; a master (teacher) could be removed from his position (called *privatio*) without being discharged from the university — a sort of suspension while his actions were investigated; likewise, a student could be suspended (*exilium*) in the same way. Both were temporarily excluded from the academic group. (Note that at this time professors and students were really not distinguished from one another in the academic group; both were scholars.)

So, to the early 1500s there had been a growth in the concept that is now called academic freedom. Around 1530, however, there began a decline in the "safety" of professors (at least in the safety of their offices). The King of France had set up the Parliament of Paris as the supreme board of governors, tribunal, of the university and began the secularization of faculties. Many religious leaders lost their positions. In 1535 Catholic scholars were expelled from the University of Tubingen, in 1539 Lutherans from Leipzig, and also in 1539 even Protestant *suspects* were expelled from Vienna. This was relatively temporary, however, and the shift from doctrinal schools to secular universities in Europe, accompanied by the shift toward speculation and research, led to reinstatement of the old immunity for scholars. Commonly, the faculties governed and policed themselves and a professor holding a chair held it for life (*durante vita*), barring serious offenses.

American colonial colleges were instituted for very specific purposes, initially religious, and there was essentially no academic freedom. Recall that Henry Dunster, first president of Harvard, had to resign when he adopted Baptist views, flaunting the Puritan teachings of the college. Yale's 1745 laws included the requirement that students could not attend religious services other than those officially approved by the president. Professors at William and Mary had to subscribe to the 39 Articles of the Church of England all the way up to the Revolution. But the general movement from the beginning was toward increasing freedom. Columbia and Brown admitted students of any religion. Pennsylvania had men from the major religious denominations on its board of governors in 1779. At the University of Virginia, Thomas Jefferson called for recognition of the "illimitable freedom of the human mind." He said that the university would not be afraid to follow truth or to combat error and would remain free to do both. But, (1) he himself mistrusted the federalists enough that he had the board of visitors prescribe the readings for the course on government, and (2) he was unable to get Thomas Cooper, an unorthodox liberal with "materialistic opinions," seated on the faculty because of religious opposition.

An early president at Brown, Elisha Andrews, opposed the gold standard for currency when his trustees favored it. Asked not to speak publicly on his views, he resigned, but he was reinstated after a public outcry. At Stanford, Edward Ross was dismissed when he spoke in favor of municipal ownership of street railways and criticized the immigration allowances for Orientals. Mrs. Leland Stanford controlled the finances of the university and she demanded Ross's dismissal. (We will hear of Edward Ross again.)

What might be considered turning points with respect to academic freedom in America were the cases of Richard Ely and of Scott Nearing. Ely was a professor of economics at Wisconsin. Having published articles on labor problems, corporate abuses, and socialism, he was accused of fomenting public unrest, which there was at the time (1893) because of the depression. A committee of the regents was appointed to investigate the charges and found Ely innocent. Instead of dismissing Ely, the regents issued a strong statement in favor of academic freedom at Wisconsin. Nearing was dismissed from the University of Pennsylvania after a one-year appointment, and no reasons for the dismissal were given. Speculation said that it was due to his liberal social views. The case served to bring to the fore the fact that professors were employees and could be hired and fired at will.

William Rainey Harper declared that the freedom of a professor to teach must not be abridged because, if it could be, his teaching would be suspect. Charles W. Eliot held the same belief, but he also felt that benefactors of the university deserved "fair treatment." Nicholas Murray Butler, of Columbia, denied over $9 million worth of proferred gifts because of strings attached. After a time in America, freedom within academia seemed not too much to expect, but there was the question of whether this freedom extended into the outside world. After all, freedom to investigate, to do research, could lead to consequences outside the university. President Lowell of Harvard felt that there was no special freedom for professors outside the university. John Dewey's pragmatism certainly did not recognize these boundaries, however. And George S. Counts went still further in "Dare the Schools Build a New Social Order?"

In addition to the general evolution of academic freedom in America, changes can also be attributed to:

    a. Jefferson's initial ideas,
    b. Darwin and the growth of science,
    c. the influence of German universities,

    d. the social Darwinism of William Graham Sumner, includ-
       ing Counts' extension, and
    e. the American Association of University Professors (AAUP).

The rise of true universities in America was concomitant with the growth of science. This correlation was certainly not coincidental, although it had not required such a drastic step as the publication of *Origin of Species* to produce the universities of Europe. With the rise of scientific research and the devotion of professors to the search for new truths, the ideas of academic freedom also came to the fore. In many early institutions there were sharp conflicts between the entrenched secular managers (trustees or presidents as the case might be) and those who sought to move the universities away from sectarianism and toward unregulated research and teaching. Alexander Winchell was a professor of zoology and geology at Vanderbilt when he wrote a piece on the evolution of man in 1878. Vanderbilt was not yet ready for full university status and Winchell was dismissed; he was almost immediately hired at Michigan, however.

William Graham Sumner was a sociologist at Yale under the presidency of Noah Porter. He decided to adopt Herbert Spencer's book, *The Study of Sociology*, as a textbook. Spencer was strongly scientific in his orientation (and secular) and this offended Porter. However, Sumner was powerful enough, and well liked enough, that he managed to win the argument, although he did withdraw the book from his classes.

Following the dismissal (actually the resignation under duress) of Edward Ross at Stanford, the American Economics Association made a study of the case. They conducted a thorough investigation and could find no reason for the dismissal, but they found that nothing could be done about it (this was in 1901). A young Stanford professor, Arthur Lovejoy, resigned over the situation and moved to Johns Hopkins. In 1911 John M. Mecklin was similarly forced out of Lafayette College. The American Philosophical Association and the American Psychological Association appointed a joint committee to investigate, with Arthur Lovejoy as chairman. Lafayette College officials refused to cooperate in the investigation; the committee found in favor of Mecklin and the college was severely censured.

In 1913 the American Economics Association, the American Sociological Society, and the American Political Science Association, through a committee headed by John Dewey and Arthur Lovejoy, called a meeting to form a professional organization to protect academic freedom. This meeting was attended by 867 professors from 60 institutions. Amid considerable opposition, the AAUP pronounced a set of principles in 1915 as follows:

1. Professors deal with sources of knowledge.
2. Discharge of this function must be free of irrelevant factors.
3. Any termination of a professorial appointment must be based on peer judgments.
4. The university is an "intellectual experiment station" as well as a conservator of past information.
5. Professors must be free to broadcast the results of experimentation.
6. Professors, on the other hand, must:
   a. be true scholars (use proper research methods and not "jump to conclusions"),
   b. be fair in presenting their own views to present also opposing views,
   c. discipline themselves (and each other) regarding academic behavior,
   d. avoid "hasty or unverified or exaggerated statements" in public and "refrain from intemperate or sensational modes of expression."

The proposed practical procedures for colleges were:

1. action by faculty committees on reappointments
2. definition of tenure
   a. definite terms of appointment
   b. permanence after 10 years
   c. notice of non-reappointment (three months for instructors, one year for higher ranks)
3. formulation of the legitimate grounds for dismissal
4. judicial hearings before dismissal, by faculty senates or faculties at large with outside evaluations allowed.

Ultimately, the AAUP position statements were essentially adopted by the Association of American Colleges, the Association of American Universities, the National Education Association, the American Civil Liberties Union, and the American Federation of Teachers.

The AAUP was formed in 1915 — during the First World War — and the principles of academic freedom which this organization stated were called into question as to their applicability under periods of war or other national stress. President A. Lawrence Lowell of Harvard spoke strongly in favor of the principles, in particular of the idea that a professor must be free to teach as he chose within his classes and laboratories while being constrained to act as any other citizen outside the classroom. President Nicholas Murray Butler of Columbia, however, felt that war negated these principles and required unswerving allegiance to the country, even if this resulted in the temporary loss of academic freedom. Under Butler, James McKeen Cattell was dismissed for his rebellious actions and Charles A. Beard resigned in protest.

In 1925 the AAUP in conference with the Association of American Colleges issued a statement of principles replacing the earlier one. The major changes were:

a. retreat from the trial process
b. retreat from written statement of charges for dismissal
c. recognition that limited appointments (such as visiting professorships) did not require the same diligence as regular appointments
d. recognition of "financial exigency" as a legitimate cause for dismissal.

Thus, the distinction between tenured and non-tenured faculty with respect to academic freedom began to develop. If one was on a tenure-track position, he had more academic freedom, in effect, than if he was on a visiting appointment; likewise, if one had already achieved tenure and dismissal was the only way he could be gotten rid of, he had more freedom than if he had not yet attained tenure and could be dismissed by merely not being reappointed.

In a 1940 statement, the AAUP introduced practical routinization of job security, in the civil service model, with probation, application of three years of probation at one institution to the probationary period at another, setting of three-year and six-year evaluation terms, and requirements of cause for all dismissals (the latter a re-emphasis). Shortly after this, in World War II, the major question of loyalty oaths arose. In roughly the decade of the 1950s, academic freedom was in grave danger; even though the Oklahoma and Washington loyalty oaths were found unconstitutional, California and other states persisted in trying to weed out communists from university faculties through similar oaths. The United States Supreme Court, in four cases, recognized academic freedom as a substantive and procedural right. In *Sweezey v. New Hampshire*, Sweezey, dismissed because of pleading the Fifth Amendment, was reinstated.

As mentioned above, the practical review periods for professors came to be three and six years. Because of the one-year notice rule, the time during which one could remain an untenured professor was seven years. Where did the three years and the seven years come from? In 1697 Increase Mather of Harvard proposed to limit the term of a tutor to seven years and this proposal was adopted; this early regulation may have been the basis for the later seven-year rule. Some have harked back to biblical times when Jacob had to labor seven years for Leah (and another seven for Rachel) and said that this provided the basis for the AAUP specification. In truth, the original 10 years period in the first AAUP principles was eventually judged as too long. Also, as the AAUP accumulated funds, it could afford to contest more cases in court and it simply reduced the term by three years. Once the basic seven-year period had been settled upon, six years became the evaluation term (because of the one-year notice requirement) and so half of that (three years) was set as the first evaluation time.

The principles under which universities now operate were enunciated in 1970. They include:

a. Professors are responsible for seeking truth through critical self-discipline and intellectual honesty. A professor's subsidiary interests must not hamper his freedom of inquiry.
b. Professors must respect students and serve as models for them. They must evaluate fairly, hold relationships confidential, and protect the academic freedom of students.
c. Professors may criticize one another but only with respect to academic matters and in a manner respectful of the opinions and findings of each other.
d. Professors must observe the rules of their institution, seeking to change them if they are found inappropriate, and must be effective teachers and scholars.

e. The speaking or acting of a professor as a private citizen must be done without conveying the impression that the institution is being represented thereby.

f. Professors are free to present truth as they see it but must (1) present opposing views as well and (2) not present unrelated views or material.

g. Tenure is guaranteed after a probationary period for full-time professors until retirement age or dismissal for (1) financial exigency, (2) incompetence, or (3) moral turpitude.

h. Continuation of tenure involves maintenance of competence as a teacher and scholar.

In two recent court cases, the tenure situation has been clarified a bit. David Roth was hired at a state college in Wisconsin, spent a year on probation, and was not reappointed. No reasons were given for the non-reappointment. In *Board of Regents of the State Colleges of Wisconsin v. Roth*, the U.S. Supreme Court ruled that Roth was not entitled to reasons. The effect of this ruling has been that a non-tenured professor can be "dismissed" during his probationary period by simple non-reappointment and no reasons need be given. However, the time during which this procedure will be acceptable is limited. Robert Sinderman was employed for five years at Odessa Junior College in Texas and then he was not reappointed for the sixth year. Sinderman claimed discrimination because of his active role in the Texas Junior College Teachers Association, and in *Charles R. Perry* (Odessa Junior College) *v. Robert Sinderman*, the Supreme Court ruled that he was, in fact, tenured by reason of "expectation of re-employment" as outlined in the college faculty guide.

Harvard is one of the few universities that do not follow the AAUP guidelines with respect to hiring and tenure. It hires assistant professors with no expectation of tenuring them; most are employed for three years but some for as long as nine years. The university rarely promotes from within the faculty but rather hires outside scholars to replace retiring (or deceased) tenured faculty in professorships — hiring them on tenure. Most institutions, however, follow the AAUP guidelines scrupulously and they have become the practical guardian of academic freedom in America.

CHAPTER 8

MODERN UNIVERSITIES

BETWEEN the Civil War and World War II, the college student population grew about five times as fast as the population of the country. By 1940 a bachelor's degree had become the common level of education for most white-collar jobs and the professions. College was essentially open to anyone. In 1964, 40 percent of the 18-21 year age group were in college; between 1950 and 1960 the population of the country grew 8 percent while the college population grew 40 percent. Much of this growth was due to the establishment of the junior college. William Rainey Harper had set up Chicago with "collegiate" and "university" levels (the first two and last two years of the undergraduate four-year curriculum), but actually Michigan, Minnesota, and Cornell had used the 2 − 2 distinction before him. High schools were improving steadily, and there were proposals at Illinois, Michigan, and Stanford to do away with the first two years of college. Various educational ladders were tried:

$8 - 4 - 2 -$ university $(2 \ +$ graduate school$)$
$6 - 3 - 3 - 2 -$ university
$6 - 6 - 2 -$ university

At Minnesota, around 1870, the first two years of college were part of the high school in one of the following arrangements:

$8 - 6 -$ university
$6 - 3 - 5 -$ university
$6 - 4 - 4 -$ university

However, these patterns were not, apparently, set up in the public schools, only at the university for experimental purposes.

142

Robert Hutchins proposed to make Chicago into a 6—4—4—university plan, with the second four years being a four-year college incorporating the eleventh and twelfth grades of high school with the freshman and sophomore years of college and capped by a B.S. degree. Nearly everyone objected to this plan.

Harper had come to call the "collegiate" years at Chicago the "junior college" and the second two years the "senior college." With his encouragement, the board of education of Joliet, Illinois added grades thirteen and fourteen to its high school in 1902 and so started the first real (public) junior college in today's sense. Following the Joliet lead, many schools added two years and many colleges dropped their junior and senior years and became junior colleges. In addition, many private junior colleges were also founded, so that by 1920 there were 52 junior colleges in the country. By 1941 there were 610; by 1970, 1,100; by 1974, 1,141; and by 1978, 1,193.

The vocational aspects of junior college curricula expanded rapidly after World War II, and in the 1960s the move to call these institutions community colleges was prominent. Most of the 1,200 community colleges in America today offer an A.A. degree as a terminal degree, as well as offering a two-year program for advanced admission into a four-year college.

In 1926 Rollins College opened in Winter Park, Florida. The college was actually there since 1886, but in 1926 it underwent drastic changes so that it was essentially a new institution. Its thesis was that leisure is fundamental to the full development of one's self. Thus, there was no homework, classes were small (10 students) and devoted to study of the "eternal problems and interests of man," and a conference with a professor and a tennis match with a friend were of equal importance. Meanwhile, Swarthmore had introduced an elaborate honors system in 1922 with the colloquium at its heart. And Reed College (Portland, Oregon) had opened in 1912 requiring a senior thesis and an oral defense of the thesis before conferring the bachelor's degree. And Antioch College set up its alternating work-study program to help students not only to earn their way through college but also to relate the worlds of work and study to each other. (I have mentioned all three of these earlier.)

Bennington College (women's college in Vermont, 1932) tried to close the gaps between work and play, between classroom and theater, between classroom and poetry journal, etc. It also chose not Ph.D.'s but professors who had "full lives of significant experiences" outside of academia for its instructors.

Post World War II, the GI Bill resulted in huge numbers of adults demanding relevant college courses. This led to a great expansion of technical education (most of the new students wanted to learn job skills) and particularly in the growth of extension offerings. Universities recognized the existence of the extensive market that the GI Bill provided for their services and they reacted by taking the courses to the students whenever possible. Purdue University, for example, widely expanded its technical extension division; it also moved into the field (a new field) of offering courses through the broadcast medium. A DC-3 airplane carrying a huge antenna flew over central Indiana and broadcast courses to be taken by persons in their own homes.

In the 1960s the cry for relevance took many turns. There were the objections to research that could enhance war efforts — such research was seen as irrelevant to men's lives. There were the calls for special area studies such as "black studies." There were the complaints about depersonalized instruction either in large classes or through the use of teaching assistants. And there were the cries against grades that resulted in the pass-fail option for certain courses that is still in use. The emphasis on life experience as a "good education" gave rise to all sorts of plans for giving degree credit for skills acquired (or information acquired) in life activities — perhaps the only legitimate one among them being competency testing. Nova University (Fort Lauderdale, Florida) offered a doctorate off campus, mostly through independent study, but also utilizing as instructors locally situated persons around the country.

As the United States grew into a global power, its universities also acquired global significance. American outposts of higher education have been established in Turkey, Lebanon, Syria, Africa, China, Japan, and Egypt. Thousands of students from other countries study in our colleges and hundreds of U.S. professors spend time teaching and doing research in foreign institutions. In 1972, 32,148 American students were in other countries; in 1978 the number of foreign students in American colleges was over 235,000, the largest number from Iran (16%), then the Orient and Nigeria, Canada (6%), and Venezuela (4%).

So we have a very diverse set of offerings in higher education, large continuing education programs, still expanding community colleges, the leisure schools as described above, the Institute for Advanced Study at Princeton, and the massive state universities and systems (California, Texas, Florida). We have moved back toward (1) basic liberal arts studies, (2) specific vocational studies, (3) applied research, and (4) good teaching as an emphasis in considerations for promotion and tenure. But American higher education is not at equilibrium. Financial cutbacks in the wake of a faltering economy have reduced many institutions to smaller entities than they once were or have caused them to scramble for new students and new sources of income. Population shifts have had much the same result. In other instances, population shifts or mere growth have resulted in the addition of new institutions. (The university where I am writing this book has been here only eleven years; the University of Texas at San Antonio, now with some 12,000 students, opened with no students — only faculty — in Spring 1973.)

Under the leadership of Frank Lombardino, who was later referred to by President Peter Flawn as the "Father of UTSA," the Texas legislature passed a measure in June 1969 that created the University of Texas at San Antonio, the University of Texas at Dallas, and the University of Texas of the Permian Basis. (Actually, the bill was *signed* on June 5.) the UTSA was, according to this legislation, to be a semi-autonomous unit of the University of Texas System and it was to serve both undergraduate and graduate students, offering courses leading to bachelor's, master's, and doctor's degrees. This was the first time in over forty years that Texas had established a completely new institution of higher education. Not only that, but the move was made in a time when universities in other parts of the country were being forced to cut back on programs because of shortages in funding, reductions in foundation grants, and slowdowns in student enrollments.

In May 1970 a 600-acre site north of San Antonio was accepted by the regents and Arleigh B. Templeton was appointed as the first president of the institution. Under Templeton, a master plan for the campus was developed and accepted by the regents. Building began in May 1972. Meanwhile, work had been going on also on degree programs and other organizational matters; these were approved by the regents and the coordinating board in spring 1972, also, and the university actually began operating in rented facilities. The first graduate students were enrolled in the summer terms 1973. Although Doctor Templeton had moved from the UTSA to the University of Texas at El Paso in spring 1973 and Peter T. Flawn had succeeded him as UTSA president, the first Graduate Catalog contained this statement by Dr. Templeton:*

> This Graduate Catalog is the first official academic publication of The University of Texas at San Antonio. As such, it does not necessarily reflect in all details either the format or content of succeeding editions, when the University will have become fully operational on its permanent campus. It does, however, contain the information necessary for a prospective graduate student to plan his particular degree programs with the aid of administrative and faculty advice and to become acquainted with many of the procedures and regulations that are vital to the efficient service the University will strive to provide.
>
> As a new institution, operating in temporary facilities for its first year, the University will be undergoing a type of learning process along with its initial student body. Consequently, it is to be expected that modifications will be made in some of the operational procedures and regulations, always in an effort to serve the students more effectively and to function with greater administrative efficiency.
>
> This Catalog is of great importance to the beginning UTSA graduate student; of equal importance is the availability of the University's staff for personal consultation regarding any questions whatsoever. It is my personal commitment that UTSA be a student-oriented institution in the best possible sense of the term, and I encourage you to telephone or to visit personally those members of our staff who can be most helpful in connection with your interest in UTSA.

Notice the "personal commitment" portion of this statement. In the informational section of the catalog this point was also emphasized, saying that the faculty (at that point mostly still not hired) would be selected "above all else, on the basis of excellence in teaching, which is to be an institutional hallmark."

---

*The University of Texas at San Antonio, Graduate Catlog 1973-1974, p. 3.

The new university was also intended to operate collegially; it was the stated intent that there be a community of scholars to include both professors and students with the idea that each could learn from the other. And it was intended primarily to serve the San Antonio and South Texas area, although the catalog statement did not exclude a much broader reputation's being sought. The school opened with 671 master's degree students in June 1973, opened to undergraduate students on a sliding arrangement (first juniors and seniors and then underclassmen later) in 1975, and had grown to some 12,000 students by spring 1984.

The 1974-75 Graduate Catalog, under President Peter T. Flawn, made the statement that the university was committed to excellence in teaching and scholarship and thus began the transition from a primarily teaching emphasis to a modified emphasis on this part of university life with an increasing emphasis on scholarship. Under its third president, James W. Wagener, the university's 1982-84 catalog lists the following components which would seem to contribute heavily toward a research emphasis: (1) computing resources through which "faculty research (is) facilitated," (2) The Center for Studies in Business, Economics, and Human Resources, (3) Center for Archeological Research, (4) Center for Applied Research and Technology, (5) Center for Learning and Development Research in Education, and (6) Research Center for the Arts. There is also an Office of Contracts and Grants to help with this aspect of research, and the university has begun a program of internal funding of small research projects (or seed projects).

In 1984 the University of Texas at San Antonio still did not offer programs leading to the Ph.D. (or any other doctorate). The 1969 legislation had specified that the usual degrees (bachelor's, master's, and doctor's) should be offered by the UTSA, but the coordinating board has not yet approved a doctoral proposal.

Public school teachers in early America were little better educated, when they finished their schooling, than the students whom they taught. That is, a grammar school teacher commonly had a grammar school education, for example, and the expectation was that this same education was to be imparted to students in the school. In the early nineteenth century there were normal schools offering a long-term preparation for teachers and institutes offering chatauqua-type programs of a few week's duration. These institutions commonly accepted students without any higher qualifications than elementary school graduation, and so they were hardly colleges. Immediately after the Civil War, several Midwestern universities established professorships of pedagogy. Iowa and Michigan had departments for the preparation of teachers, and Columbia had Teachers College beginning in 1892. Prior to this time the normal schools accounted for a very small percentage of actual teachers, but as the universities took on the job of preparing teachers two things happened: (1) the program became more substantial, requiring in the neighborhood of two years of study, and (2) more and more it came to be expected that a teacher would have had university training before assuming a school position.

The first normal school (for teachers) was opened in Concord, Vermont in 1823; this was a private school, the first public normal school began in 1839 in Lexington, Massachusetts. The lateness of these dates suggests that teacher preparation was not highly regarded in our early history. However, once the preparation of teachers began, it grew rapidly (as did most movements in higher education in America). By 1890 there were 92 normal schools supported by public funds. Following World War I there was a period of growth again so that by 1931, 75 percent of elementary school teachers had at least two years of training and three out of five junior high and high school teachers had four years of training.

The growth of high schools resulted in the normal schools' transition to institutions that required high school diplomas for admission, and with this change the institutions themselves moved toward becoming four-year colleges and toward granting degrees to their graduates. Normal schools became teachers colleges, and before long teachers colleges became state colleges and many later became state universities. (In Indiana there was Indiana State Normal School, which became Indiana State Teachers College and then Indiana State University; Ball State Teachers College became Ball State University and is on the way toward becoming a major university in the sense of having a medical school as well as the usual colleges. In Illinois there was a similar pattern. Four regional normal schools and a major normal school, Illinois State Normal University, first prepared the state's teachers. Then all of these became state teachers colleges, then state colleges, and finally state universities. And the same story could be told of many other states.

A few former teachers colleges merged with state universities or became branches of these universities. This followed the intrusion into teacher education of the universities, most of which have established departments, divisions, or colleges of teacher education. Teachers College-Columbia University, Harvard, and the University of Chicago have only graduate programs for teachers.

Not a large number of new universities has been added in the past decade or so. The state of higher education since the late 1960s has been such that it was more likely that some institutions would fail rather than new ones being established. Potential students were not going to college (for various reasons), state legislatures were cutting back on appropriations, funding for grants and outside contracts was "drying up," and the climate was just not good for growth among institutions of higher education. There were some changes that moved colleges into other systems — for example, the George Peabody College for Teachers in Nashville, Tennessee, became an undergraduate division of Vanderbilt University. There was also some broadening of existing university branches into full-scale universities; the University of Alabama at Huntsville and the University of Alabama at Birmingham are examples.

Alabama also established a completely new institution, a regional state university at Mobile, called the University of South Alabama; this was in 1963. The Federal City College in the District of Columbia became a land-grant college in 1968, but this was not a new institution. Alaska became a state in 1959 and its University of Alaska (Fairbanks, with branches at Anchorage and Juneau) became the youngest of the major state universities, but it had been founded as the Alaska Agricultural College and School of Mines in 1922. Hawaii's newest college is Hawaii Loa College near Honolulu, founded in 1963. This is a church-sponsored college (four bodies); the University of Hawaii goes back to 1907 when it began as a college of agriculture and mechanic arts.

Presently, the higher education systems in New York are the City University of New York and the State University of New York. The former has existed since 1847 but the latter only since 1948. The city colleges which preceded the City University of New York (nine of them including Hunter College, which opened in 1870 as the Female Normal and High school, and six city junior colleges — one in each borough) were managed under the state commissioner of education by the New York City Board of Higher Education. The colleges operated separately until 1961, but under the same management board, and at that time the City University was established. The university is city tax supported but receives state subsidies as well. New York State established the University of the State of New York as its total program of formal education, all levels, both public and private. The president of the University of the State of New York and state board of regents becomes (or is) the state commissioner of education. Outside the city of New York this body has traditionally managed (that is, overseen) public education, with emphasis on the elementary and secondary schools and on private colleges, and the public colleges developed only slowly. The A & M components of state higher education were operated by Cornell University, although they were located on state-owned campuses adjacent to Cornell. There were teachers colleges, managed under the state board of education, but the medical schools and most other higher education were in private universities.

Under Governor Thomas E. Dewey, the legislature in 1948 established the Board of Trustees of the State University of New York to exercise jurisdiction over the state institutions and, presumably, to oversee the development of the system, which at that point was largely undeveloped. The state university, of course, was not an institution at all but merely an assembly of disparate colleges and schools. However, in 1962 the University of Buffalo was acquired by the state (it had been a private institution) and became the first unit of the state university, the State University of New York at Buffalo. Warren Bennis described its proposed development into a veritable "Berkeley of the East" in an article published in 1972.* Bennis was invited by the president of SUNY at Buffalo, Martin Meyerson, to

---

*Warren Bennis, "The Sociology of Institutions of Who Sank the Yellow Submarine?" *Psychology Today* (November 1972): 113-120.

serve as one of the provosts who would oversee the transformation of this school into Meyerson's dream of a 30-college new campus with action research centers and with highly qualified professors and top-student undergraduates. According to Bennis, the major problems that prevented this dream from becoming an immediate reality were related to the lag of the funding for buildings and programs behind the recruitment of faculty and the admission of students. All of the dream programs had to operate in crowded quarters, and in this setting the new programs were unable to attract the prominent scholars desired and so disaffection grew to huge proportions. Meyerson (and Bennis) left Buffalo in 1970 and the institution reverted to essentially what it had been earlier. Under state mangement, however, it did slowly develop its own reputation and its graduate programs achieved favorable evaluation by the American Council on Education.

Two medical colleges and the State Universities of New York at Albany, at Binghamton, and at Stony Brook, plus a number of community colleges, now constitute SUNY. The board of trustees is, in effect, between the university and the regents, but, in fact, this board manages the system.

The public universities in Florida had been of long standing: the University of Florida which began as East Florida Seminary in 1853 (Gainesville), Florida State University which began as West Florida Seminary for Women in 1857 (Tallahassee), and Florida A & M University which began as Florida State Normal School for Colored Students in 1887 (Tallahassee — no more than three miles from Florida State University). The state university system was vastly expanded in the 1960s and early 1970s by the addition of Florida Atlantic University at Boca Raton (1961), the University of West Florida at Pensacola (1963), the University of North Florida at Jacksonville (1965), the University of Central Florida (which began as Florida Technological University) in Orlando in 1968, and Florida International University in Miami (1972). In addition, the University of South Florida at Tampa had been separately established in 1960. The state is also full of private institutions, many of a specialized nature. Nova University opened in 1964 as a private institution that offers a great number of off-campus programs, including doctoral degrees.

For some time the University of Illinois had a branch operation (small scale) at Navy Pier in Chicago. In 1965 this unit was moved to a campus southwest of the Loop and designated the Congress Circle campus of the University of Illinois. The name was later changed to the U of I, Chicago Circle and still later to the University of Illinois at Chicago, a name that places it on par with its older sister downstate at Urbana-Champaign. The Chicago campus is dominated by the 28-story University Hall, Chicago Circle Center, and one of the largest medical centers in the world with a 16-story College of Nursing and a 500-bed hospital. Prior to September 1982 UIC had two campuses separated by a portion of the business-residential area in which the university was earlier planted.

The university and the community have interacted in many ways over the years to the point where the campus has largely been accepted as a part of the environment rather than an alien presence. In 1982 this integration was aided by the joining of the two campuses into a single unit and by construction of the Pavilion, a sports and entertainment complex just across the street from a large shopping mall. UIC is reported to have the largest enrollment of all colleges in the Chicago area.

As a closing note for this chapter, not all is rosy in the college/university picture today in America. Major institutions in northern states have had to cut back drastically in some of their programs because of funding decreases and also because of declining enrollments. The university expansion in Florida described above resulted in, perhaps, an oversupply of institutions for the available students. This system too has suffered budget cuts and declining enrollments. Among the colleges that find themselves in the most awkward positions, however, are those institutions that began as black colleges.

Fisk University in Nashville, Tennessee*, has dropped in enrollment from a high of 1,125 to 694 in 1984. Fisk was founded in 1866 and flourished as one of the best of the black colleges, along with Howard University (founded 1867). Now its endowment funds have been depleted, it has a debt of some $2.8 million, and it has had to raise its tuition to $6,800 per year for board, room, and tuition charges. (The problems of Fisk and of other black colleges stem from the efforts of formerly "white" institutions to entice the best black students into their courses in order to meet federal requirements. At the same time, previously black colleges that have tried to integrate also have been largely unsuccessful.)

---

*Kilpatrick, James J. "Casualty of Changing Times." (San Antonio, Texas: San Antonio Express, June 12, 1984).

CHAPTER 9

GOVERNANCE PATTERNS

T HE universitas of European education was essentially a guild. The scholars united and pretty well managed their own affairs. However, presidents or chancellors soon came into being as the administrative leaders. Lay control existed in the person of whatever ruler chartered the school — emperor, king, pope, bishop, elector. In America the chartering agency was the British Crown (if asked, e.g., in the case of William and Mary) or the local authority (e.g., the General Court of Massachusetts in the case of Harvard). In either case it was the practice to set up a supervisory board, usually called overseers, governors, or visitors, and later regents, to provide lay control. This lay control tradition had been adopted from Scottish institutions, but in many, if not most, of the early American colleges "lay" was not the correct term. The trustees in the colonial colleges were clergymen (e.g., Rhode Island College had a board composed of 22 Baptists 4 Congregationalists, 5 Friends or Quakers, and 5 Episcopalians).

Boards became secularized as the colleges turned toward secular education. By 1860 about one-fifth of boards consisted of businessmen; by 1930 it was one-third. In 1860 only 5 percent of boards were educators; this increased to 10 percent by 1930. Faculty members on boards (and even students on boards) have been proposed for many years but were rarely appointed until recently. It would seem that this practice goes against the basic purpose of the board, that is, lay control.

Hofstadter and Hardy* attribute to the lack of a "teaching class" the designation by the founders of Harvard of a board of overseers consisting of six magistrates and six clergymen. In the magistrates, of course, there was the foundation of the current lay boards of regents and in the clergymen there was the foundation of what was to be clergy control of colleges essentially throughout the pre-Civil War period. Whether it is indicative of what might have been or whether it is the result of what was, it has not been popular in recent years (and it did not occur at all before that as indicated above) to have teachers on boards of control of universities. In other words, it seems doubtful that, had there been a "teaching class," it would have been members of this group that were assigned to manage the colonial colleges. The religious fervor of the times, the very reason for America being colonized, probably would have (and did, in my view) led to clergymen on boards of control. As a matter of fact, it is a bit odd that the number of magistrates on the Harvard board were equal to the number of clergymen until one considers the basic distrust of clergymen by the Puritans.

At any rate, the Harvard Board of Overseers ran the college until 1642 when it became the permanent external governing body. The only faculty person on the board was the college president; this pattern was followed at most of the colonial institutions, but in later years the board did not include presidents. The precedent for separate lay and faculty governing groups was also set at Harvard. In the 1650 charter there was established the corporation, which was to consist of the president and fellows of the college, whose actions had to be approved by the board of overseers. Remember that fellows in the colonial colleges did not necessarily mean professors (or teachers); it included other scholars (students) along with the teachers. Thus, the actual Harvard Corporation was intended to have the college president, the treasurer, three or four teaching fellows, and one or two students (or learner fellows). In practice it was not even exactly this way. Since there were only a very small number of tutors in the college, the corporation consisted most of the time of the two officers named above, two teaching fellows, and three former fellows

---

*From Richard Hofstadter and C. DeWitt Hardy: *The Development and Scope of Higher Education in the United States.* 3rd ptg., (New York: Columbia University Press, 1963).

who by the time of their service were practicing ministers. Thus, the teachers really had very little to say in the management of Harvard.

As the college grew so that more tutors could be employed, the practice of having only two tutors on the corporation continued. Eventually even this number was reduced and finally there were no longer any teachers on the corporation. What then developed was a new "outside" board (the corporation) that virtually replaced the board of overseers.

The founders of William and Mary set up an outside governing board, called the board of visitors, consisting of four ministers and fourteen laymen. But they also set up the William and Mary Corporation consisting of the president and masters of the college, and this corporation was not reduced either in number of members or in constitution. Thus, William and Mary was pretty well managed by the faculty. Actually, the board of visitors was scheduled to decline in authority and did so to 1729, when it gave up all of its authority. Between that time and the Revolutionary War, the college was managed by its faculty. After the war a new charter was set up (since the charter of William and Mary had been a *royal* charter) and this reconstituted the board of visitors and made it the controlling body.

At Yale the board of trustees, which in this case did not include the college president, had absolute governing authority. It was empowered to employ the president and, of course, the faculty and to make all other substantial decisions regarding the operation of the school. (The president — rector — was made a member, indeed chairman, of the regents later — in 1723 and 1745, respectively.) This same pattern of governance was followed at Princeton and has remained as the predominant one for universities until the present. Typically, today there is a board of regents that holds the authority over financial matters and also the final authority over even academic matters. It has the power to hire and dismiss the president; it has the authority to grant or deny tenure upon the recommendation of the president, so it holds authority over individual faculty members; and it is actually this board that awards degrees, so that it has authority over the students as well. More or less matching the corporation of earlier colleges, most institutions have a faculty senate (sometimes called by other names) which makes internal academic decisions. Frequently, these decisions are not interfered with by the regents, but very often they are subject to approval of the president and then the regents. Even if the approval extends only to the president, remember that the regents can hire and fire this person, so, in effect, his/her decisions are under the scrutiny of the regents in any case.

Members of the early college boards of governance, as was indicated above, were largely clergymen. Over the years this gradually changed so that clergymen were replaced by businessmen and politicians — businessmen because they were needed to help with the increasing financial needs of institutions, and politicians because most of the boards of public institutions were appointed by governors who can wield their own influence by appointing cronies (or persons who hold the views they want to have promulgated). So the boards of governors of our educational institutions consist of persons who typically know about as much about education as you and I know about medicine (we are influenced by it, we benefit from it, we even practice it in very amateurish ways on our children — would this qualify us to be managers of a hospital?).

In 1870 the U.S. Bureau of Education was listing "colleges" in the country. This was only an informational list and not an evaluation. However, there was the natural question of whether or not a given institution should be listed as a college, and there was also a bit of pressure from the "better schools" for the bureau to evaluate institutions and thus to make the listing a sort of accreditation. Rather than getting involved in doing this as a government agency, the bureau asked the Carnegie Foundation to make the evaluations. The foundation made a study but declined to publish lists, so the colleges themselves formed a kind of mutual accreditation group: the North Central Association of Colleges and Secondary Schools (1894). Later on, other regional accreditation associations were formed.

In 1905 the University of Berlin asked the Association of American Universities to tell it which colleges could send graduates to Berlin who might be expected to do the work required. Beginning in 1914 the AAU did publish accreditation lists (until 1948). The states also have accrediting agencies as do various professional associations, such as the American Chemical Society. But the federal government does not accredit colleges today, just as it refused to do at the beginning.

The presidents of colonial colleges were clergymen, head teachers, and overseers of all aspects of college life. As colleges grew, subordinate administrators became necessary, a librarian (at first, the president was also the librarian), then a registrar, deans (ca. 1890), other assistants in the 1900s, and then vice presidents in the mid-1900s. The clergyman president was unable to cope with the growing secularism of colleges, and often scientists replaced him. Gilman of Johns Hopkins was a geographer, Eliot of Harvard a chemist, Hall of Clark a psychologist, Jordan of Stanford a biologist, and Barnard of Columbia a chemist/mathematician. Woodrow Wilson was the first real lay president of Princeton.

More recently, presidents have been either:

    a. scientists as above (Flawn of the University of Texas)
    b. scholars from other fields (Wells of Indiana)
    c. prominent persons (Eisenhauer of Columbia)
    d. "money getters" or
    e. effective managers

The faculty role in administration has changed over time. In the colonial colleges the corporation was, presumably, managed by faculty. But as presidential powers grew, actual faculty power declined. Faculty senates replaced the corporation as the real mode for faculty input in governance, and senates have been powerful or weak, depending upon circumstances. In recent years the faculty role has declined and the presidential role has increased in power.

Unless the person is ineffective and retiring, a university president shapes the university to his/her own pattern. Regardless of the philosophy of the institution and of the existing structures, when a new individual has assumed the leadership and has had some time (usually several years) to exert influence upon curriculum, courses, administrative patterns, and faculty activities, the institution will change subtly, or not so subtly, to reflect the president's views. If this is not the case, except as noted above, the president will probably leave the institution. In recent history, Herman Wells certainly shaped Indiana University and the same is true with James Bryant Conant of Harvard. Under David Dodds Henry, the University of Illinois was a most collegial institution, and under J. Stanley Marshall, Florida State University was decidedly not collegial. The new University of Texas at San Antonio began under president Arleigh Templeton as a tightly run organization designed to utilize modern technology in courses and to be an institution known for its quality instruction. Under Templeton's successors, Peter Flawn and James Wagener, that emphasis has changed first toward a much heavier research component and then toward a modified research-teaching viewpoint.

Woodrow Wilson was a graduate of Princeton (1879). He studied law at Virginia and then went into the graduate school at Johns Hopkins from where he received his Ph.D. in 1885. He was a professor at Bryn Mawr and at Wesleyan and then at his alma mater, Princeton. He was the first non-clergyman to become president of that college (in 1902). Although later in our history presidents of the United States might move on to become university presidents, Wilson was a university president before entering into his political career; as a matter of fact, it was his work at Princeton that brought him into the public eye.

Many of the great names among early college presidents are essentially from the same era, from immediately after the Civil War until early 1900. Specifically, one could point to Charles William Eliot of Harvard as the perfector of the elective system, to Noah Porter of Yale and James McCosh of Princeton as those who opposed the elective system most vehemently and logically, to Frederick A.P. Barnard of Columbia as a leader in the co-education movement, to Daniel Coit Gilman of Johns Hopkins as the visionary who instituted true graduate work in America, to Andrew White of Cornell as the leader who made "land grant" into a very positive term in higher education, to William Rainey Harper of Chicago as a leader in numerous areas, and to others as well. The following is a list of institutional presidents who were active in the era noted.*

---

*Vesey, Laurence R., *The Emergence of the American University*, (Chicago: The University of Chicago Press, 1965).

Charles William Eliot — Harvard	1869-1909
Noah Porter — Yale	1871-1886
Timothy Dwight — Yale	1886-1899
James McCosh — Princeton	1886-1888
Frederick A.P. Barnard — Columbia	1865-1889
Daniel Coit Gilman — California	1872-1875
— Johns Hopkins	1876-1901
Andrew White — Cornell	1871-1888
James B. Angell — Michigan	1871-1910
William Rainey Harper — Chicago	1892-1906
Charles R. Van Hise — Wisconsin	1903-1911
David Starr Jordan — Stanford	1891-1911

Each of these men certainly left his mark on the university he headed as well as in higher education in a more general way in America.

It would appear that to be a university president one needs to have three names (at least) or an initial and a middle name. Look at the triple names: Andrew Dickson White of Cornell, James Burrill Angell of Michigan, William Rainey Harper of Chicago, Robert Maynard Hutchins of Chicago (1929-1951), David Starr Jordan of Stanford, James Bryant Conant of Harvard (1933-1953), Charles William Eliot of Harvard, Nicholas Murray Butler of Columbia, Daniel Coit Gilman of Johns Hopkins, Hanna Holburn Gray of Chicago (presently). And look at the initial plus middle-name presidents: G. Stanley Hall of Clark, A. Lawrence Lowell of Harvard, J. Stanley Marshall of Florida State, A. Bartlett Giametti of Yale (presently), and G. Armour Craig (presently acting president of Amherst).

Notice a president who had two middle names, Frederick Agustus Porter Barnard of Columbia, and some who used a first name and middle initial: Charles R. VanHise of Wisconsin, Arleigh B. Templeton of the University of Texas at San Antonio, and Peter T. Flawn of the University of Texas at Austin. Finally, there were a few college presidents who used only their first and last names: Noah Porter of Yale, Timothy Dwight of Yale, James McCosh of Princeton, Woodrow Wilson of Princeton, Ira Remsen of Johns Hopkins (another chemist, by the way), Derek Bok of Harvard (presently), Logan Wilson of the University of Texas at Austin.

If having two or three names besides a surname is a prerequisite to becoming a college president, then I stand a good chance of moving up some day; my name is Paul Henry Martin Westmeyer. (Perhaps unfortunately for presidential dignity, my wife has a different interpretation of my middle initials, H.M.)

Today, individual institutions are finding more and more that they cannot remain independent of other neighboring institutions. In some cases this has resulted in cooperative agreements among colleges so that a student at one institution can take courses for transfer credit at another in the group. In other cases the cooperation has been imposed by coordinating boards, a sort of superboard placed above the boards of regents in a state (Texas, Oklahoma, California, Illinois, and Wisconsin at least have powerful "superboards"). In still other cases, even states have agreed to combine efforts in higher education; the Southern Regional Education Board (1949) involves sixteen southern and border states in a pact of cooperation.

Institutions of higher education have probably always proliferated when there was a market that they could tap. Similarly, programs within institutions have probably proliferated as long as there were students who would take them. We have seen that some of the changes that came about during the evolution and decline of the elective system worked to the good of higher education and some to the bad; if anyone had been able to predict which would turn out to be the latter, they probably would have been avoided. States have attempted to "foreguess" competition and supply-demand conditions in higher education by establishing (whatever they might be called in various locations) superboards to regulate their colleges and universities. M.M. Chambers decries this move rather eloquently as follows.*

> The...thrust toward bundling the governance of all or many of a state's public universities and colleges into the hands of one state-wide governing board, or the alternative of superimposing a power-laden "coordinating board," deserves...careful examina-

---

*M.M. Chambers, *Higher Education in the Fifty States.* (Danville, Illinois: The Interstate Printers and Publishers, Inc., 1970).

tion and monitoring. To the extent that this movement diminishes or destroys the autonomy of the university or college by removing decision-making from the campus to the statehouse or some other remote point, creating a species of "absentee landlordism," it tends to short-change and insult the constituency, and to debase the institutions.

To be sure, the interests of all the people of the state are superior to those of any institutional constituency; but state-wide public interest can be well served without the power-play involved in the abolition of governing boards or their reduction to impotency. The solution is in the limiting of the state-wide central agency to the work of facilitating interinstitutional *liaison*, performing data-gathering, research reporting, making planning studies, disseminating of public information, and aiding in the representations of state-wide public higher education to the governor, the legislature, the institutional governing boards, and the general public — all in an advisory capacity and by means of permissive and persuasive methods, free of the exercise of raw power.

A state university is not properly conveived as an inanimate *mechanism* which can be operated by remote control, with Big Brother pushing the buttons on the control panel on the twentieth floor of the state office building. Instead it is a living *organism* with its own complex skeletal and muscular structure, its own circulatory and nervous systems, its own capacities for encouraging initiative and inventiveness and maintaining the atmosphere of expectancy which is most conducive toward discoveries in various fields of learning. Its morale, and its productivity, can be greatly diminished or destroyed by rude "chopping off of fingers and toes" by a power-laden "superboard."

Fear of "duplication" of general undergraduate programs is a relic of Depression days and earlier, when public higher education was a very thinly-spread enterprise. Virtually all undergraduate curriculums and courses, whatever their labels, contain large infusions of liberal arts or general education, which indeed needs to be "duplicated" (or better, diffused, diversified, and dispersed) until it is accessible to all citizens. Wariness of alleged "duplication" would have some point with respect to costly advanced graduate studies and research, were it not for the fact that the scholars and scientists who lead these enterprises are always aware of what their counterparts in other institutions in the same state, if any, are doing and planning. Within the fraternity of top-level scholars and scientists there is intercommunication often unknown to administrators and others, and on a level which would be uninteresting and unintelligible to lay citizens and even to professional persons not immediately concerned in the special fields involved. This is insurance of a sufficient degree of "coordination" without the intervention of uninformed fiscal clerks. Wise governing boards and administrators know their best service is to encourage it, not impede it or clumsily meddle with it.

Nevertheless, coordinating boards, some with awesome degrees of authority, exist in all but ten or a dozen of the states. In some the coordinating board is advisory, but in many it is a truly regulatory body. In Texas no new program can be begun and no new course can be offered without approval of the board. A program, once approved, cannot even undergo a name change without board approval. (The University of Texas at San Antonio maintains a rather strange sounding and non-descriptive program, titled "Institutions of Higher Education," because it was denied permission to change the name of the program to "Adult and Higher Education." The latter name might not have been better than the former, but the point is that the change depended upon approval of the coordinating board and this was denied.)

WRAP-UP

We have seen that colleges in young America were begun with the purpose of perpetuating the prevailing religions, indeed, of making Christians of the native Americans as well as of settlers in the New World. In comparison with European institutions, and certainly in comparison with today's American colleges and universities as well, these early schools were much more that (schools) than they were colleges. We should not put them down, however, for the country was building, it had no education system for the public, it had few if any facilities for educating youth, it was a raw frontier, and the colleges served a vital purpose. They began a tradition in this country that has grown into the great systems we have today — the University of California, the University System of Texas, the "Big Ten" universities (to utilize the sports designation), the A & M's, MIT, and the well-known private universities (Harvard, of course, Yale, and the other Ivy League schools, Stanford, Notre Dame, and others). And it all began because of the desire of the Puritans to perpetuate their beliefs AND to have an educated ministry.

Most research today, certainly most *basic* research, is done in university settings. There are, of course, research organizations attached to various industries and a few of these do indeed engage in basic research, but by and large they are for the purpose of furthering the causes of their parent industries. And this all started with the Johns Hopkins idea, except that one must not forget the contribution of Cornell both to that idea and to other aspects of university life. The fact that research in America is free, that its practitioners are neither limited in what questions they may ask nor restricted in the publication of their findings, began with an acceptance of the German ideals of *lehrfreiheit* and *lernfreiheit*, but it is really the result of

164

the activities of the AAUP. American ideals of academic freedom, indeed, have become the international ideals (with the probable exception of "iron curtain" countries).

To the sciences, of course, must go a great deal of credit for today's universities. As we have seen, the research underway in European universities long before the opening of Johns Hopkins in America was of the "philosophical type," except that the orderly collection of data was a part of it. (The modern sciences can't take credit for orderliness, at least.) Scientific research as it has now developed changed this by introduction of the experimental method in which one manipulates variables deliberately in order to observe the effect of this manipulation on a dependent variable. As the sciences developed, the nature of research questions changed; primarily, it became appropriate to question *anything*, nothing was beyond being subjected to investigation. However, it was through the sciences that the art of theorizing was developed and research then became appropriate (actually necessary) to verify theories. Thus, we have the dichotomy today between basic research (meaning research to verify theories) and applied research (meaning research to solve problems or answer questions of a non-theoretical nature). All of these aspects of research were applied not only in the scientific disciplines themselves but also in other disciplines and so "scientific research" has had a much broader application than might be supposed.

In addition to the influence on research, the sciences have become large fields of study in their own right. Information has accumulated at a tremendous rate (exponential in some areas and for a time). And, of course, the sciences have contributed personnel to college administration in rather large numbers; many college presidents have been scientists, as I have pointed out.

Could one pick an individual and say that this person has had the greatest influence on the development of higher education in this country? Well, Charles William Eliot certainly saw to it that the elective system reached a peak — a peak that turned out to be too high so that the system declined to a much more moderate one. Was it then Noah Porter and others who tried to hold the elective system in check that made the greater contribution? Since such heavy emphasis has been placed on the role of Johns Hopkins, was it Daniel Coit Gilman who made the greatest contribution? Or could it have been William Rainey Harper who took the Johns Hopkins' idea and really "ran with it" at Chicago? Certainly a lot of practices in today's universities had their beginning with Harper's institution. It may sound strange coming from a professor in the University of Texas system, but I guess that I would pick Andrew White of Cornell. (Maybe the visionary was Justin Morrill, but certainly it was White who made the A & M idea come into a reality.) The broadening of higher education started at Cornell and it was really the joint idea of White and Cornell himself. Add to this the A & M aspect of Cornell and surely the conclusion must be that there was a truly major contribution to the whole picture from that institution.

Are "new" universities different from those longer established? Have we learned from experience how to build institutions? The answer appears to be no in both cases. The recently established major universities look an awful lot like their older counterparts. The emphasis may be a bit more on teaching, but that could be an artifact of their needing to attract students more than they need to attract scholars in their beginning stages. In spite of the "technological revolution," there are still large lecture classes, small discussion classes, seminars and colloquia, and the like as there have been for many years now. True, the theories of Jean Piaget (thought to deal primarily with the learning processes in young children) have been applied in college settings with good results and true that we have done more thinking recently about why we teach adults as we do, but the effects of these have been on classes or curriculum segments rather than on structures or overall procedures. Philosophically and psychologically, we haven't changed much.

A movement not treated in any detail in this book has been so-called competency based education. Colleges within universities have tried this approach and individual institutions have been started with it as the basis for procedures. (Governor's State in the Chicago area was competency based, for example.) At this point I would have to say that the movement has not had a major effect on institutions in spite of its successes in individual programs.

Has higher education in America reached its epitome then? It could be. Basically, things are going well. Research continues to provide theories and verifications for theories, as well as answers to applicational and descriptive questions. Students continue to learn by our methods (even though they might be outdated by some standards). Professors emphasize whatever is rewarded — research, publication, teaching, advising — but professors are a breed apart and they also emphasize those intellectual pursuits which they consider important in their own right, regardless of any rewards, and this contributes to the propriety of the title, university. *Lehrfreiheit* is alive and well; *lernfreiheit*, perhaps unfortunately, has been somewhat influenced by the vocationalism of this age. Students are there not to "learn" but to acquire credentials that will enable them to obtain higher-paying jobs. This may not be bad, however; surely the strength of this country is in its people, and if the people want to better themselves the country will benefit as well. And alma maters will benefit and education will continue to grow.

Yes, everything points to growth continuing. The community colleges are expanding their programs, continuing education is becoming larger and more widespread, and more people are finding that they want degrees whether or not they need them for what they want to do (in the last sense we may be returning to some semblance of a desire for liberal education among our people). The picture is basically rosy, in spite of my comments at the end of Chapter 8.

INDEX